absolutely beautiful containers

The ABCs of Creative Container Gardens

absolutely
beautiful
containers

The ABCs of Creative Container Gardens

sue amatangelo

Ball Publishing | Batavia, Illinois

Ball Publishing
335 North River Street
Post Office Box 9
Batavia, IL 60510
www.ballpublishing.com

Cover and interior designed by Lisa Weistroffer.

The following names are registered trademarks (®) of Ball Horticultural Company: *Angelonia* 'Angelmist', *Begonia* 'Baby Wing', *Begonia* 'Dragon Wing', *Calibrachoa* 'Starlette', *Coleus* 'Kong', *Coleus* 'Wizard', *Impatiens* 'Fanfare', *Pelargonium* × *hortorum* 'Fantasia', *Pelargonium* × *hortorum* 'Showcase', *Pelargonium peltatum* 'Galleria', *Pelargonium peltatum* 'Colorcade', *Perilla* 'Magilla', *Petunia* 'Easy Wave', *Petunia* 'Tidal Wave', *Petunia* 'Wave', *Tagetes* 'Durango', *Torenia* 'Clown', *Viola* 'Bingo', *Viola* 'Matrix', *Viola* 'Panola', *Viola* 'Sorbet', *Verbena* 'Aztec'.

The following names are trademarks (™) of Ball Horticultural Company: *Antirrhinum* 'Luminaire', *Impatiens* 'Super Elfin', *Impatiens walleriana* 'Fiesta', *Lantana* 'Lucky', *Lobelia* 'Waterfall', *Nemesia* 'Aromatica', *Osteospermum* 'Serenity', *Petunia* 'Ruffle', *Petunia* 'Suncatcher', *Primula* 'Primlet', *Portulaca oleracea* 'Rio'.

Library of Congress Cataloging-in-Publication Data

Printed in Singapore by Imago.

12 11 10 09 08 07 06   1 2 3 4 5 6 7 8 9

dedication

To Steve and Nick

contents

acknowledgements

It took many hands to be able to share my love of container gardening with you, and I want to thank those that were there for me throughout my journey. To the people at Ball Horticultural, PanAmerican Seed, Ball FloraPlant, Ball Seed, and Ball Publishing who supported my efforts to put this book together, I thank you.

Ball Horticultural Company, a family-owned business founded in 1905, is an internationally renowned breeder, producer, and wholesale distributor of ornamental plants. Not only have they developed some of the best-loved varieties on the market today, they are also responsible for getting these varieties to the commercial growers who supply independent garden centers and other retailers . . . and ultimately, the home gardener. Ball has introduced many innovative, award-winning varieties to the world of horticulture, including the 'Ride The Wave' family of petunias, *Pennisetum glaucum* 'Purple Majesty' (ornamental millet), the 'Fiesta' double impatiens series, and thousands more. Ball continues to lead the industry in plant breeding, research, and distribution with worldwide production, sales, and marketing through its many subsidiaries in more than twenty countries on six continents. Wherever you go, it is likely you will find Ball plants nearby!

Special thanks to Mark Widhalm whose creative eye photographed many of the container gardens in this book that I am sure will inspire you; to the Ball Horticultural Company Advertising Department for all their help, ideas, and suggestions; and to my editor, Rick Blanchette, who never gave up on me. Some of the containers in this book were created by the very talented employees of Ball Horticultural, and I appreciate being able to share them with you.

I would also like to thank New England Pottery, Pride Garden Products, Braun Horticulture, Garden City Plastics, and Campania International for their contribution of a number of containers that you will see in this book.

Thanks also go out to the following people for allowing me to use their beautiful home settings to photograph some of the containers in this book: Bob and Julie Eberspacher, Jeff and Shelley Bauer, Ken and Mindy Blaesing, Ernest and Joanne Isadore, and Chip and Carol Hammersmith.

Most of all I would like to thank my husband, Steve, and my son, Nick, who gave up our time together as a family so that I could spend weekends and evenings working on this book. You are my inspiration!

introduction

I remember as vividly as it was yesterday my grandfather and I sitting in my mother's garden, my grandfather on an overturned bucket and me sitting in the grass, pulling weeds and talking about anything that came to our minds. Occasionally my grandfather would point out a flower that was blooming, and he would tell me a story that went along with it. Either it was some funny tale or a memory. These are very fond memories and ones that I am sure instilled my love for gardening. Today, I try to do the same for my son, showing him when a flower has bloomed or a large mushroom pops up in my garden, and having him help me plant and water my container gardens that sit on the deck, in the front of our house, and within our garden beds. I cannot think of anything better to give our children than the love and appreciation for gardening. It doesn't take very much to gain their interest. Usually your excitement in gardening will automatically filter down to them, although it may not happen for many years. It is a great time to talk, laugh, and even get messy together. Even for those resistant to succumb, I would never give up on trying to excite and capture that new gardener. I'm glad my grandfather didn't give up on me.

With our busy lifestyles and all the opportunities that our children have we find that the simpler things in life take a backseat, and traditions that had been handed down through generation after generation that connected our families are quickly disappearing. Gardening can help bring that sense of family back. Children love to play in the dirt, and gardening can be a wonderful way to teach them about nature while also creating life-long family memories. And there's nothing quite as magical as a child's wonder and excitement watching that first bloom from a flower that he planted and cared for together with you.

Why not find a little room in your life to enjoy gardening—an activity that has so many positive attributes with so little effort? Start small and simple, and if gardening was never something you thought would be of interest to you, you will be pleasantly surprised at how watching your flowers bloom will move you and make you feel like a kid again as well. What if you have the interest and the desire, but also a to-do list of chores, errands, and work that's seems never ending? With so much to do, it is hard to take time to stop and enjoy the beauty that surrounds us. Sometimes it's all we can do just to get the list done and get some rest at the end of the day. And yet studies have shown that gardening is not only one of the most popular hobbies, but it can also have a calming effect on our lives and how we view our surroundings. According to a study done by the University of Illinois, gardening has even been known to reduce crime rates. Why, I have been known to solve some of my greatest problems while spending a little bit of time in my garden . . . or if nothing else I become a calmer, happier person. In this constantly busy society, gardening is the perfect way to achieve some quiet solace and a communion with nature.

But what if your lifestyle is one that you do not have either the time or the space for gardening? How can you get in on this growing hobby that does so much good without spending so much time? That's simple . . . container gardening. Yes, even the meek and the garden "newbie" can give it a try and gain confidence, enjoyment, and the peace and tranquility that goes with the sheer enjoyment

of watching your container garden grow and come alive. Once you start, you will never look back.

Even the elderly individuals who thought they had to give up their beloved pastime because they are no longer able to get down on their hands and knees or use a shovel can rekindle their passion through container gardening. The effect is just as beautiful as a full-sized garden, and because the container stands at a higher level, this gardening is not as physically demanding. Watering and weeding is also a breeze and much easier to handle in a container than in a ground bed.

Container gardening is a fun and exciting hobby that brings color and texture to your outdoor living space. It is easy to do and will bring hours of enjoyment to you, your friends, and your family. In this book you will find recipes for containers in this book that will take you from spring to summer and right into autumn—containers that are wild and wonderful as well as easy and entertaining.

I hope you enjoy the container gardens that you see and maybe one of them will find their way onto your deck or into your garden. Come join me on this exciting endeavor and discover how fulfilling and fun container gardening really can be!

the basics of container gardening 1

Container gardening is one of the fastest growing segments of the gardening industry. Enthusiasts like you can create a little slice of container garden heaven to enjoy anywhere and at any time. You can change the look of your container garden throughout the growing season, move it around to various parts of your deck, patio, or landscape, or just bring it indoors to enjoy through the winter months. Few things in life are as easy and versatile and provide so much pleasure.

It may be hard to find anything else that is quite as easy and fun than to design a container and watch it grow up on your deck or patio. In fact, anyone that is afraid of taking the gardening plunge should give container gardening a try. It is a great way get your feet wet, build your confidence, and allow your creative side to shine. The best part is that once you've tried it, the garden bug will definitely bite you, too!

getting started

Container gardening is for everyone: the young, the old, and everyone in between, and taking your first step is easier than you may think, as long as you follow a few guidelines. First, decide where you would like to display your container garden. The location can be almost anyplace: a deck, a garden, a table, or anywhere you would like a splash of color.

Next, determine whether the location you are selecting is mostly sun, part sun/part shade, or shade. Monitor the location a couple of times during the day to see what the light levels are. You will want to keep this in mind when shopping for plants. Remember that as the spring and summer progress, the light levels may change and what was once a fairly sunny area may have more shade later in the season. Having your plants containerized will allow you to move them around to receive just the right amount of light all season long, extending the bloom time right into autumn.

Full-sun plants usually need about four hours or more of sunlight each day. Part sun/part shade will do fine with two to four hours of sunlight, and shade plants can thrive on dappled light or less than two hours of direct sunlight each day. If you find that your plants are not blooming as prolifically as when they were first planted, it could be that the plants are not receiving the amount of daily sunlight required to keep those blooms coming. Just move your container to a sunnier location, and that may take care of the problem. Or they

may need fertilizer, which we will discuss later.

Your local garden center carries plenty of beautiful flowers and colors to select from for all light requirements, so finding that ideal variety should not be difficult. If you do not find everything that you need at one shop, try another. Each garden center varies and sometimes it takes more than one stop to find that perfect plant or the perfect color that you had in mind. I have been known to make trips to three or four different garden centers to find the plant or color for which I was searching. Keep in mind that shipments and replenishments usually happen weekly, so if you are not successful this weekend, do not give up. You will have another opportunity to look at a fresh batch next week.

Assess the area that surrounds the location that you plan to display your container. Make sure that the colors from the railings of a deck or other flowers that may be in bloom will not conflict. Also look at the foliage that is already there. Will it complement the plantings in your container, or will it detract from the beauty of it?

Finally, keep the size of the container in line with your display area and with the size of plants you will be purchasing. If it's too small, it will get lost. But if it's too large, it will look out of place. A good rule of thumb is to keep the container to about one-third the total size of your finished container garden.

You can really make an impact with container gardening, and we are all looking for that "Wow!" from family, friends, and neighbors. So with that in mind, let's talk about what makes a great container garden.

selecting the container

There are two very different schools of thought on when to select your container. Some experts believe it should be the first item that you look for when you walk into a garden center, thinking about size, shape, and color. Others say it should be the last item you choose; making sure it will complement the colors of the flowers that you have selected. Quite often you may find that you come home with an entirely different container look, size, and/or shape than you originally planned. I've been known to fall in love with a container, and the next thing you know it's sitting in my backyard.

container types

You can select from among many containers in garden centers today. No longer are you confined to just two choices: terra-cotta or plastic. Ceramic, fiberglass, and metal pots are just some of the container substances readily available, along with wire baskets lined with moss or coco fiber.

Lightweight pottery has become a popular container item in garden centers. You can fill up a very attractive container and still be able to move it around easily to capture the seasonal changes in sunlight or to satisfy your need for a new look, similar to rearranging the furniture in your living room. The pots are made with a substance called fiberglass or resin, which accounts for their lightness. These choices are so attractive and well made that it is hard to distinguish the heavyweight containers that require three people to move them from the fiberglass that you can pick up with one hand. They are durable against the elements and look great year after year, both indoors and out. I have a few fiberglass pots in my garden and after six years they still look as good as when I bought them.

Another popular entry into the world of outdoor containers is the ceramic or glazed clay pottery that is being imported into the United States from places like the Philippines, Malaysia, and Singapore. These containers have a beautiful glazed finish on the outside that is not as porous as other ceramic pots, allowing the soil to retain moisture longer. The pots are available very rich tones, such as burgundy, dark blue, and topaz, providing a lot of color to the landscape. They are also offered in very large sizes, allowing you to create showcase container gardens. The drawback to these beauties is their weight, even when they are empty, so be sure to pick a location that will be more permanent for the season. Remember not to leave them out in freezing temperatures because they can crack. When you are ready to bring them indoors for the winter, you'll probably need some additional assistance to move them to their warmer resting place.

Some containers say that they are frost proof; however, anything filled with water when it freezes solid could break from the expanding ice, even certain steel, concrete, and plastic. The ice forms in the fissures or pores and strains the structure, causing expansion and pressure within the walls of the container. Some pottery, like most terra-cotta, is highly porous after the firing. However, pottery from Vietnam is fired at a very high temperature so the clay material becomes non-porous. If a container is glazed both inside and out you may think that it can withstand the freezing weather and will not crack; this is not entirely true. Quite often there are small areas of these containers missed in the glazing process or tiny cracks that allow water to seep in and swell as it freezes, weakening or damaging the container. To be safe, it is always a good idea to bring your containers—frost proof or not—into a dry area for winter storage.

Terra-cotta or unglazed clay is another popular choice that has been around for a very long time. It is, with out a doubt, one of the most common choices for container gardens and comes in many different shapes and sizes. These containers are a bit heavier than the fiberglass versions, but they have the unique ability to breathe, which is a plus for healthy roots. Keep in mind that the soil in the container will dry out a bit faster and therefore will require additional watering. This is not a benefit in areas that are under watering restrictions or experiencing drought conditions. These containers can be used year after year and will continue to look great. The drawback to terra-cotta containers is that they can crack or chip easily. As with most containers, it's important to store them in a cool dry place for

Photo courtesy of Campania International

Photo courtesy of Campania International

Relatively new to container gardening is the sleek look and lines of metal pots. You can choose from such materials as copper and aluminum. These containers provide a streamlined, modern look and are very lightweight. Unfortunately keeping some of these products clean, shiny, and attractive can require a little extra work, but the overall beauty of these containers is well worth the additional effort.

Plastic pots have been around for a long time. They are probably the most inexpensive of all containers and are also routinely used by growers to bring your plants and hanging baskets to market. These pots are very lightweight and will last for years to come. Most plastic pots resist breakage and fading and are recyclable. And it is becoming harder to distinguish the plastic terra-cotta from the real thing. Plastic companies have been taking plastic pots to the next level, producing containers that are lightweight, inexpensive, and more attractive than ordinary plastic pots. They can be brought home from the store and placed directly on your deck or patio allowing you to skip the planting part. When the season is over, these pots can be stored to use again next year or recycled.

You will find almost all hanging baskets in plastic containers since they are extremely lightweight, and the plastic manufacturers have dressed up the look of these containers allowing you to bring your selection home and hang it right up. These days, you can find plastic hanging baskets in one of three basic colors—white, green, and

the winter to extend the life of the container. Be careful when transporting your terra-cotta containers to avoid chipping.

Do you want to add some color to your terra-cotta pots? Then get out the paint, brushes, and sponges. Stripes, dots, diamonds, or any pattern will add a colorful touch to your container. If you are a teacher, a parent, or a grandparent, you can decorate your container with pint-sized handprints. This fun and creative activity will make a memory that the children and you can enjoy year after year.

terra-cotta. Some retail locations will use the colors of the hanging baskets to determine how much the basket will cost based on the more upscale and expensive products in the basket. So be aware that there might be a price difference when you arrive at the cash register with your selections.

Additional container substances that are beautiful but not as drought-tolerant friendly are the coir- or coco-, moss-, and grass-lined wire baskets, which can be found at many upscale garden centers. Coir is fiber from coconut husks and is natural and organic, which makes it a good choice if you are looking for something that is environmentally friendly. This material lines the sides and base of a wire basket and soil and plants are added. Although the airflow is great and the roots can breathe easier, the basket tends to dry out very fast requiring water at least once, if not two or three times a day. The windier the day, the more you'll be out there with your sprinkling can or hose. These containers are usually in the form of hanging baskets or window boxes, but new looks are coming out all the time. You will see several examples of wire baskets in the following chapters. If you like the look of a grass or coco hanging basket, buy one that has a built-in water tray system that helps the basket to stay moist. This tray will capture excess water and hold it like a reservoir to be drawn up by the roots when needed. You can also mix water-absorbing crystals into the container mix before you plant to help reduce the amount of times that you may have to water.

Photo courtesy of Pride Garden Products

Photo courtesy of Campania International

Cast iron has been around for many years, is very heavy, and comes in various urn shapes. At the end of the season it is important to protect these containers from the elements to extend their life, but it may be difficult to move them due to their weight. Other types of containers available are made from granite, precast concrete, sandstone, wicker, or wood and are all great containers to use. Each adds a different feeling, element, and flair. Some are more casual like wood, while others such as cast iron will definitely give a very elegant, formal look. Many of these materials are even heavier than the glazed ceramic pots or will need additional attention each year to keep them looking their best, so choose wisely.

saucers

When you plan to take your summer vacation and find that you do not have anyone to care for your container gardens or are unable to move them into the path of the automatic sprinkler, you can use a saucer underneath the container. Buy the next size larger saucer than your container so that the water uptake will not be restricted. Just before you leave to go out of town, water your plant and then fill up the tray with water. This should hold water for a couple of days, giving the plant a drink when needed.

In areas where there are drought conditions, you can also place saucers or trays under all of your container gardens to catch any water runoff and hold it in the tray. This will keep the plants hydrated

as well as offer an often-needed humid environment at the base of the plant. However, if the weather is extremely hot, try to move your containers into a shady area of your deck, patio, or garden every now and then to give them a break from the intense heat.

pot risers

If you do not like the look of the round circles that appear on your deck when you move your containers into storage at the end of the season, you can purchase a few feet or pot risers. These are ceramic or terra-cotta pieces that fit under your container and allow water that wants to drain out of your container to move freely away from the bottom and not pool around your container. This will keep your deck dry and prevent it from becoming stained.

Photo courtesy of Campania International

dress it up

Don't forget all the creative items you can add to your container garden. Garden art is a wonderful addition to your container that provides an element of fun and surprise. Any item from your home will work and can be placed in or next to the container. Candles, a sleeping angel or a bird house . . . whatever you have on hand, can become a part of a container garden. There are so many clever things you can do not only with the containers that are used, but also with the way they are displayed or decorated. It is amazing how you can change the look of a container garden just by adding something as simple as curly willow branches. Do not limit your creativity when it comes to container gardening. Who knows? It just may be the next big trend!

The addition of a bumblebee or dragonfly can create an element of surprise in your container.

A paint-can garden with blooming plants can also make a great gift for a neighbor or friend who is in the middle of redecorating or remodeling a home and is in need of something colorful to raise their spirits.

Be creative and have fun with your choice of container. Try using a birdbath, a stoneware crock, an old boot, or the hollowed-out inside of a tree stump. Imagine what a conversation piece you will have by using a straw hat turned upside down or an old purse sitting on top of your patio table with flowers flowing out of it. You do not even have to take time to plant if you use a decorative birdcage or watering can. A carpenter's toolbox can be used to make an instant container garden, or an old-time milk carrier could be lined with coco fiber for planting. With these creative containers, you can just drop the plant, in its original plastic pot, right into the attractive container that you have chosen and you are done.

For example, new, unused paint cans are a quick, fun way to add color to your shade garden. Purchase the paint cans at your local craft store, and then simply drop a pot of impatiens or other plant variety into the can. You will have a charming display that will last for a few weeks. Use packing peanuts or a small pot flipped upside down in the bottom of the can, if you need to boost the level of your plant.

When you are ready to buy your container, you may choose to purchase a style that comes in more than one size, rather than trying to match two or more different containers in different sizes and colors. Not only will this save you time when shopping, but you will be able to store these containers inside one another. Planting your matching container will be a snap. You can follow three different roads when planting: Plant one color or one variety in each container,

Want a real show-stopping container? Try these partial faces. Add a short grass to the back of your arrangement, and you'll have a wild-looking container that will bring a smile to anyone who passes.

mixing up the varieties or colors so that each container includes the same contents and complements one another or make each container totally different. The fun comes in when you are ready to display your containers. You can cluster the pots together on a deck, in a garden, or on a patio, separate them and place each in a different location, or place them together on the steps of your porch. When clustering your containers, you could also plant a dwarf tree that has a lot of definition and/or color in a large pot. A Japanese maple would be a beautiful pick and will look great as the backdrop to two or three other matching containers. You can even use items such as overturned pots to prop some of the containers up giving them height and allowing each container to really stand out on its own. When you get tired of the look, any or all of the pots can be moved to a new location.

inside the container

When selecting your container, there are a few details to check before making your purchase. Doing a quick inspection could save you time and expense in the long run. First and most important is a drainage hole. Most plants are not overly fond of wet feet; think of how your feet would feel if they were sitting in water for a long period of time. One of the worse things you can do to your plants is leave a pool of standing water in the bottom of your pot because the excess water has no place to go. Eventually, the water will build up and create a top-to-bottom mud ball. I have had this happen to me, and it

Photo courtesy of Campania International

is a hard lesson to learn when you end up losing the plants in your container and have a muddy mess to clean up. Wet soils prevent good aeration and nutrient uptake and can lead to root rot and other problems with bacteria. Some gardeners fill the base of the pot with 2 inches of gravel or smash soda cans and place them inside the bottom of the pot to create a place that can collect the water away from the plant roots. However, in my experience, at least one drainage hole in your pot is necessary.

If a drainage hole is not included, then consider the type of pot you are buying and whether or not you will be able to add one. You will have no problem adding drainage to the bottom of a fiberglass pot by using a large nail and hammer. However, putting a hole in the bottom of a ceramic container is a bit trickier. An electric drill with a masonry bit is the tool to use, but you have to be patient. If you are even a little bit hasty, you can end up cracking the entire container.

To help make containers lighter, you can break apart a Styrofoam board or add packing peanuts to the bottom half of the container and cover that with a piece of burlap, adding the soil over the top of the burlap. This trick will make your containers substantially lighter and still allow the water to drain. When you are done for the season and ready to clean out your pots, the burlap will keep the Styrofoam from flying all over your backyard or garage.

Also, when you bring your plants home from the store, instead of throwing the plastic packs or pots into the recycling bin, why not put a few upside down in the bottom of your container garden to reduce the amount of soil that you will need to use? Even imprinted pots can be used in your containers without fear of harming your plants. Cover the pots with potting soil and then plant as usual. When it is time to store your container at the end of the season, recycle the plastic pots.

If you are using a large container and plan to use a tall, heavy plant in the container, do not use plastic pots or Styrofoam as fillers, since the container will be top heavy and could easily blow over. Instead, place one or two bricks at the bottom of the container, being careful not to cover the drainage holes, before filling with potting soil.

When you have chosen the perfect container to bring home with you, take a moment to check the inside of any breakable containers for small, hairline cracks. Often, these cracks will not be readily visible on the outside of the pot and if left in the changing elements the container can swell and break. If the container is lightly bumped in transit to the patio or porch it could actually fall apart. Steer clear of any damaged container with a clearance tag on it because even the smallest crack can mean reduced longevity and will be no bargain in the long run.

soil

Soil is important to understand and is vital for the success of your container garden. It can make the difference between a so-so presentation and a spectacular look. It is best to refrain from heading out to your backyard to scoop up the dirt from your garden to fill your container. Field soil or the soil in your backyard is much too heavy for the roots of your plants, making it difficult for them to move and breathe. The soil may also contain diseases or viruses and little critters that can take their toll on certain varieties. This could slow the growth of the plants in your container and possibly cause damage. Clay and/or sand are usually a major ingredient in backyard soil and are present in quantities that do not provide a good growing environment for your plants.

Buying topsoil at your local store is also not the way to go. Instead, look for the bags labeled as container mixes. These mixtures are usually made of many things but not soil, which is why they are often referred to as soilless mixes. The ingredients are the perfect blend for the health and growth of your plants and are free of viruses and pests. Bark, perlite, and vermiculite are typical ingredients, and many mixes will also contain a starter charge of fertilizers. These mixes will hold water, retain air, and provide the proper pH for healthy plants. Some mixes will even include moisture-retaining crystals (see the Saving Water sidebar).

Soilless mixes are very lightweight. You will be able to pick up a large bag quite easily and carry it out to your car, without the assistance of a store clerk. If you find a bag is difficult to lift, chances are it is not the right type of mix you for your container garden.

saving water

If you are looking for a way to reduce the amount of watering that you have to do, there are products on the market that can be added to the soil before planting that will help retain the water in your container a little bit longer. This crystal, gel-like substance, called a synthetic acrylic polymer, acts like a sponge, absorbing water that would otherwise have run out the drainage holes, and holds on to the moisture to release it when the soil begins to dry. It also helps the aeration of your soil because it expands and contracts each time you water the container, and that's also good for your roots. The gel will need to be added before planting your container, distributing it throughout the potting mix for it to work properly. Adding it on top of the mix once the plants are in the container will only lead to a gooey mess. Some of the products on the market today even include fertilizer. Read the instructions on the package to make sure you've added the proper amount for the size of container you are using. Although this will help to keep your plants moist longer, you must be careful not to think that it will substantially reduce or eliminate your need to water your containers.

Another way to dress up your container garden and eliminate some watering is to add a layer of stones, mulch, or sphagnum moss to the top of the container when you are done planting. The stones or pea gravel can be purchased in several different colors that can match your pot or décor. Mulch is available in course to finely shredded material and will break down as the summer progresses to provide additional nutrients to the soil. The addition of a natural layer of mulch, stones, or sphagnum moss will help to reduce water evaporation, prevent the splashing of dirt onto the lower leaves, and give a beautiful look to your container garden.

It is always best to read the ingredients on the bag before you buy.

After planting up your container and watering it for several days or weeks, the soil in your container can begin to become compacted. Give your roots a "breather" by using a trowel to gently loosen the soil in your container.

Can you use the soil left in your container from last year? It is really not a good idea. If want your container garden to be the best it can be, then it's important to give it every advantage that you possibly can right from the start. Leftover soil has decomposing roots that can rob new plants of nitrogen. In addition, there could be diseases harboring in the soil and they are just waiting to get their microscopic hands on the fresh stock that you are about to plant. Help your plants by providing them with an environment that is nutrient rich from the beginning, and you will definitely be rewarded with a healthy, beautiful container garden.

fertilizer

Although you may prefer not to fertilize your garden beds for environmental reasons, you should fertilize your container gardens, as they have limited resources from which to draw nutrients. Fertilizing your container garden can mean the difference between a nice-looking container garden and one that really draws attention. Plus, adding the right fertilizer to a struggling plant can provide it with a stronger base on which to build and help it regain good health.

The three basic, non-mineral elements that are vital for life and readily supplied by Mother Nature are hydrogen, oxygen, and carbon. These abundant elements can be found in the air and water. Plants automatically take up the amount that they need of each and, with the energy from the sun, covert these nutrients into starches and sugars, which become the plants' food. However, not all nutrients are as readily available as carbon, oxygen, and hydrogen, which is why you will need to add fertilizer to your shopping list.

There are plenty of plant foods to choose from at your local garden center. In fact there are so many that it may be a bit perplexing. When shopping for a fertilizer, you will typically find a series of numbers on the package label, such as 10-15-10, 10-10-10, or 45-10-14. The numbers will usually be in sets of three and have a meaning that you will need to understand to get the best performance out of your fertilizer and plants. Do not be intimidated by the numbers. They simply relate to three different elements that are needed for the all-around good health and well being of your plants and the percentage of each that is found in that bag or box.

These elements are nitrogen, phosphorus, and potassium. These primary nutrients, or macronutrients, are needed in the largest amount by plants but may be the least available in the soil. Plants need you to routinely provide a fertilizer that contains these nutrients, particularly in your container garden where there is little opportunity to acquire these nutrients from the surrounding soil.

Nitrogen (N) is the first of the three numbers and is essential for leaf growth, making leaves lush and strong. The leaves absorb sunlight to manufacture food for the plant through photosynthesis. The more leaves the plant has and the larger their surface, the more photosynthesis can do its job to feed the plant.

Phosphorus (P), the second number, is for flower production as well as fruit and root development. The flower is the most visually desirable part of the plant and the more blooms on your plant the happier you will be. The bloom is actually the reproductive organ. The root system acts as an anchor for your plant, is a place of storage for food and absorbs moisture and nutrients. The better the root development, the stronger your plant will be.

The third number is for potassium (K), or potash, which promotes the overall hardiness and disease resistance of your plants. This can help your plant through stressful situations, such as extreme heat, drought, and diseases. It will also increase flower size and color.

Secondary macronutrients that you may see listed are calcium, magnesium, and sulfur. These nutrients work by helping in functions such as seed production and the uptake of nutrients. They are usually found in sufficient amounts in the soil and are not always needed as a supplement.

Finally, trace elements, or micronutrients, are those elements that are needed for good plant growth but are required in small amounts. Elements such as boron, chlorine, and copper fall into this category

reasons to fertilize

- Yellowing leaves
- Recently transplanted plants
- No blooms
- Stress
- Stronger roots
- Overall health and well being of the plants

and typically do not require a separate application.

Now that we know what it all means, how do we select the correct fertilizer? A general, all-purpose fertilizer is usually a good choice for routine needs. Look for a set of three equal numbers on the package, such as 10-10-10 or 17-17-17; these are a great pick no matter what the brand or where you buy it. One exception is when you want to encourage your plants to produce flower buds during times when the growth rate of most plants slow down; then you may try applying a fertilizer that is higher in phosphorus.

Fertilizer does come in a couple of different forms. Most dry and liquid forms are usually concentrated and will require a bit of mixing before use. Leftover diluted concentrate plant food can be stored for use later or shared with a neighbor. Some fertilizers are ready for use, so it's important that you ready the label carefully. Hose-end sprayers that mix the proper amount of chemical with water as you apply it work great for both fertilizers and insecticides. However, although they are very easy to use, they can be quite costly.

You may want to try organic fertilizers. These are very user friendly, and there is really no danger of damage to the roots and/or plant. The drawback is that they are usually more expensive and sometimes leave you in doubt as to how much you really applied due to their varying levels of nutrients. Usually when this happens you end up going to a chemical application. Apply organic fertilizers according to their individual package directions and take the time to understand the amount of additional effort it will take to go organic.

For a healthy and beautiful container garden, routine fertilization is a must. You can adhere to one of two basic fertilization routines that will fit into your summer schedule: once every six to eight weeks or every two weeks.

A six- to eight-week fertilization regiment requires selecting and mixing a time-release (also referred to as extended-release or slow-release) fertilizer into the soil before planting and then adding a supplementary application, as recommended on the package, working it directly into the soil. An application once every two to three months is suitable for most container gardens. Time-release

fertilizers come in a shaker bottle but usually include a measuring spoon for more exact measuring. For example, in the northern climates, mix a slow-release fertilizer into the soil before planting in April, and then add more in July, working it into the soil; this will take you through to the end of the growing season. You can find time-release fertilizers at any garden center in several sizes and brands. Read the directions carefully to guide you to the perfect amount of slow-release fertilizer that will be needed for each of your containers. The directions will also indicate how to apply the fertilizer and how often.

Many gardeners choose to apply their fertilizer on a two- to three-week schedule, feeling that they have more control of the care and feeding of their plants. These fertilizers are typically fast acting, and the nutrients are readily available when the plants need them. This practice usually requires mixing liquid or dry fertilizer in water and adding it via a watering can or a hose-end sprayer to the plants. When using this route of fertilization, be careful to apply as directed to avoid root damage. Some fertilizers can be applied to both the soil for rapid uptake by the roots and the leaves, allowing additional absorption of the plant food. However, if you are uncertain or feel uncomfortable with this practice, then applying the fertilizer directly to the soil is the best route to take.

The weather can also play a part in the amount and rate of fertilizer consumption or degradation Ask your local garden center employee if the local weather conditions are impacting the fertilizing of their plants and what they are doing to correct or compensate.

If you are ever in doubt, applying less fertilizer is by far better than too much, which can end up damaging your plants. Call or visit your local university extension office to get answers to your questions about fertilizing. Always store chemicals in a cool and dry location and keep them out of the direct sunlight, and always read the back of the fertilizer label carefully before applying to your plants. Be sure to keep them out of the reach of children.

plants

Once you have picked out your container, think about its size and make sure the plants that you select are proportional to the container and suited for the lighting in the area and season. If your container is a particular color or colors, select plants that will complement the container rather than clash with the color. For example, pottery from Mexico or the Southwest can be highly colorful, you may choose flowers of a single color to complement with these multicolored containers. Mixing too many colors can look like a three-ring circus with no place for the eye to settle and enjoy.

Read the back of a plant's tag to find out if it prefers sun, part sun/part shade, or shade. If the tag is missing, do not be afraid to ask the garden center employees for information or an extra copy of the tag. The tag can also help you determine how tall the plant will grow, how wide, and if it prefers the cooler days of spring or hotter days of summer.

These tags have a tremendous amount of useful information and may even direct you to a Web site where you can find out more details about the plant you have selected. Gardeners typically stick these tags into the soil next to the plant after it is put into the ground for future reference. In a container garden, you may find it easier and more attractive to group all the tags for the varieties in a container together and place them in the soil in an inconspicuous place at the back of the planting. That way you will not accidentally break the leaves, flowers, and/or stems when reaching for the tags.

You may also use a photo album with sticky pages to keep the tags in order after the summer to keep track of your favorite varieties and those that performed well for the following year. You may also take a picture of a completed container and include it with the corresponding tags to remind you of a combination that you liked or the individual plants that did not do well and would need to be swapped for another variety.

When shopping for your plants you will notice that the choices can include annuals, perennials, or biennials. Garden centers usually keep these categories separate, and it's not very often that you will ever see a biennial category called out. In general, annuals are plants whose seeds are sown in the spring. They flower all season, dieback in the fall, and they generally do not return the following year.

Perennials will winter over and continue to return for three or more years. Most perennials have a specific time when they will bloom and once that time is complete you will only be able to enjoy the leafy portion of the plant. However, there are a few perennials available that once they begin to bloom will continue to produce flowers right up to the very first frost in autumn, such as *Corydalis lutea* and *Coreopsis* 'Moonbeam'. Perennials typically are more expensive than annuals because of the extra time that it takes to bring them to market.

Depending on where you live a perennial can actually be an annual and an annual, a perennial. If you are in the market to use a perennial in your container garden with the thought that you will plant it in your garden bed later for the following year, then you will need to pay close attention to the USDA Hardiness Zone that is listed on the plant tag. Every area of the United States has a zone number assigned to it. This is a plant hardiness zone and is based on a zone map produced by the United States Department of Agriculture (USDA) to determine a plant's ability to make it through the winter months and bloom again the following year. The further north you go, the smaller the numbers become. For example, Chicago is in Zone 5. Zone 5 includes any area whose average winter temperature minimums are from −10 to 20° F. Thus, if a gardener in Chicago wanted a perennial to return the following year, she would have to purchase a plant that is perennial to Zone 5 or less. If she selects an item that is a perennial to Zone 7, then the chances are pretty good that she will not see it return again next year.

If you are not really crazy about the leaves that are left after your perennials have completed their bloom cycle, you can always remove the spent perennial and replace it with another attractive blooming or yet-to-bloom variety. (If that perennial is within your USDA Hardiness Zone, plant it in your garden bed, so that you can enjoy it next year.) You can look at this rotation of plants in your container as an opportunity to slightly change the look by adding another annual or perennial for the rest of the season. No rule says that whatever you plant in the spring must stay there until fall. Therefore when a plant starts to look a bit tired, it gives us a chance to breathe new life and excitement into the container by replacing it with a new look, whether it is annual or perennial.

To rotate plants, just take a hand-shovel and dig into the soil all around the plant that is to be removed. You can also work your fingers into the soil to loosen the roots and gently lift out the plant. If it is your intention to replant the item you removed into your garden bed, then you will want to do that soon after removing it from the container. Remove the replacement plant from its pot and massage the roots a bit to loosen the soil. This should help you to fit the plant into the vacated space. Once the new plant is in place, add additional soil and press down gently. Water to remove any possible air pockets and refresh the roots.

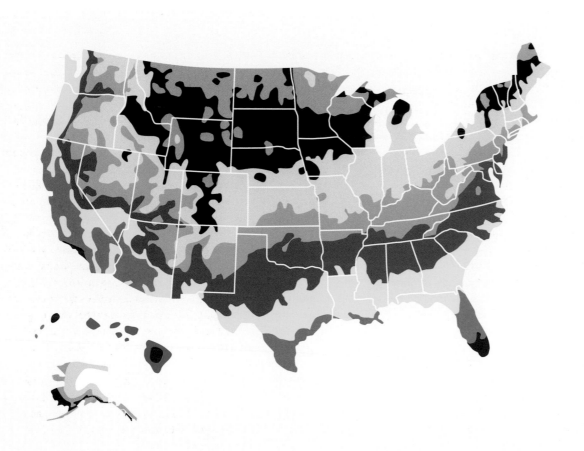

plant hardiness zone map

zones are based on the following
average minimum temperatures

zone 1	below −50° F
zone 2	−50° to −40° F
zone 3	−40° to −30° F
zone 4	−30° to −20° F
zone 5	−20° to −10° F
zone 6	−10° to 0° F
zone 7	0° to 10° F
zone 8	10° to 20° F
zone 9	20° to 30° F
zone 10	30° to 40° F
zone 11	above 40° F

Plants known as biennials require two years to complete their growth and bloom cycle. Seeds are sown in the spring and a rosette-type base plant will be all that appears the first season. The following year, after they receive a cold winter treatment, they will bloom. Foxglove is an example of a biennial. If you are not sure if you have selected a biennial in its first or second year of growth, do not place it in your container garden. It is quite possible that you could be looking at a rosette all summer long without any blooms to enjoy.

Many traditional container gardeners limit themselves to all annuals. They plant, grow, and, when the first frost came, put their containers into storage, discarding anything that is left. Container gardens do not have to be limited to just annuals or perennials. Why not enjoy the splendor of a beautiful perennial in your container garden or even the addition of an herb? Don't be limited by the categories—mix them up and have fun. Choose as you desire, and don't be afraid to be daring.

create a plan-o-gram

One way to approach the design of your container garden is with a plan-o-gram. Retailers use carefully designed plan-o-grams when creating displays in their stores to attract their customers. Plan-o-grams show the installer where and how the display should be set up as well as all the components that are needed all on a piece of paper. I like to think of a plan-o-gram as my recipe for gardening.

You can develop a plan-o-gram on paper or in your mind's eye. A container garden plan-o-gram helps give you a direction to head before entering the garden center as well as a list of varieties and the amount of each that you will need to purchase. This could save you time and eliminate what could be a confusing and frustrating trip to the garden center.

Draw the shape of the top of your container on a piece of paper and note if you are planting a sun, part sun/part shade, or shade container. On the side write down the plants that you would like to put in that container giving each a number or letter. Write that number/letter inside the container drawing to determine plant placement and decide how many plants of each variety you will need. Next make a list of additional products or items that you will need to purchase to completely prepare the container garden, such as fertilizer and container mix. Take this drawing and list with you to the garden center to remind you of all the components that you will need to buy. The last thing that you want to do is to get your selections home, realize that you forgot something, and have to make that trip all the way back to the garden center. See the example on page 20.

For some of us it is necessary to see the items before making our selection or have the item in hand before we can make a decision. In that case, take your empty or partially filled in plan-o-gram with you to the store. Select your container, carefully place the plants that you would like to purchase inside the container, and move the pots around until you are happy with the look. This visual will also help you determine if you have over- or underestimated the amount of plants you will need to fill your container. Jot down on your plan-o-gram just how you arranged the plants as well as the varieties that you have selected. Completing the plan-o-gram in the garden center will help you to recreate your design when you arrive home and facilitate assembling your planter.

varieties

a *Impatiens* 'Fiesta' (2)

b *Coleus* 'Kong' (2)

c *Alternanthera* 'Purple Knight' (2)

supplies   Container mix (1 large bag), gloves, 10-10-10 fertilizer, container

plan-o-gram worksheet

date

container size

light

a _____

b _____

c _____

d _____

e _____

container mix

fertilizer

gloves

room to grow or instant impact?

Gardeners typically take two different routes when planting their container gardens: Leave room to grow or enjoy instant impact. Each route depends on your personal philosophy and/or where you live.

In the South, with its long growing season, smaller plants can be purchased and additional room can be left around the plants to allow them to naturally grow together over time. This method requires patience and is very effective, allowing the roots and plants ample time and room to grow and get adjusted to their neighbors.

In northern areas of the United States, the growing and enjoyment season is fairly short, so planting for instant impact is more common. This requires additional or larger plants and the ability to squeeze the selected plants together. This method is also great if you're having a party on the deck or in the garden and you need some color quickly. Creating an instant-impact combination will give the impression that this container garden has been growing all season long. These plants will do well for a while but eventually may compete for space. With this method you can create one look in the early part of the season when certain varieties are shining; then as they begin to fade, replace them with varieties that are better suited to the upcoming season. This allows you to enjoy the container throughout spring and summer . . . by autumn you may have a totally different look and feel from that first spring planting.

tall or upright plants

- Ornamental millet
- Geraniums
- Argyranthemums
- Alocasias
- Colocasias
- Caladiums
- Dracaena
- *Perilla* 'Magilla'
- Hibiscus

selecting your plants

Most 10- to 12-inch containers will hold three medium-sized plants. In the garden center you'll find most medium-sized plants in pots that are 4, 5, or 6 inches across the top. These are good sizes to use in your combination planting. If they are any smaller, you will wait all summer for your container to fill in. If they are any larger, you might be hard pressed to squeeze all three plants into the same container. The plants' pot shape—round or square—has absolutely no bearing on how the plants were grown or how they will perform.

When selecting your plants at the garden center or when preparing your plan-o-gram for your 10- to 12-inch container always look for one plant of each type to create a well-balanced container garden: a tall or upright variety (U), a mounding variety (M), and a trailing variety (T).

If your container is larger than 10 to 12 inches, use two or three pots of each growing habit. If you need only one more variety to fill the container, then decide which habit you prefer. If you like the trailing variety best, then purchase an extra trailer to fill that empty space. If you like the look of more blooms, then add one more of whatever variety is your favorite. It is what you like best that will allow you to enjoy your combination most throughout the season.

Tall or upright (U) plants usually take center stage in most container gardens. They include varieties such as ornamental millet or *Perilla* 'Magilla'. You can also use a trellised plant, such as *Thunbergia alata* 'Sunny' or mandevilla, as the tall or upright plant. The wider or taller the container, the taller your upright plant can be. You can even use plants such as *Musa* spp. (banana tree) or palm trees for the very center of a very large container. These wonderful tropicals have become more affordable and very popular for all types of gardening, especially in places where you would not expect to see a banana or palm tree. You may even cut down the banana tree at the end of the season, bring it indoors, and have a new plant the following spring to incorporate into your container gardens again.

Sometimes secondary uprights are needed in larger containers to give an additional tier and full-looking container. In this case geraniums, celosia, pentas, and salvia all work well.

mounding plants

- Impatiens
- Marigold
- Begonia
- Torenia
- Coleus
- *Calathea* spp.
- Hosta

Mounding varieties pretty much stay where you have planted them and will fill in the area around the top of the container.

Trailing plants fill in the empty spaces and grow over the sides of the container. They are plants on the move and at times may need to be trimmed or pointed in the right direction. You can find trailers that add an accent with their foliage or trailers that bloom and add color.

Some plants can be considered both mounding and trailing or mounding and upright simply based on their growth habit. A good example of this would be *Petunia* 'Easy Wave'. This variety will mound and trail allowing it to not only fill in the empty spaces of your container garden but also trail over the sides.

An old-time favorite that is a perfect example of the tall, mounding, trailing concept is the spike, geranium, and vinca combo. The spike is the tall variety, which provides height to the center of the container.

trailing plants

- Ivy
- *Dichondra* 'Silver Falls'
- *Dichondra* 'Emerald Falls'
- *Ipomoea* spp. (ornamental sweet potato vine)
- Trailing impatiens
- Calibrachoa
- *Iresine* spp.
- *Petunia* 'Wave'

The geranium, although a bit tall, is still shorter than the spike and is considered the mounding variety; it fills in the open spaces around the spike beautifully. Finally, the vinca is the ideal the trailing plant. When looking for additional fillers, dusty miller is always a great choice.

Now, if you are an instant-impact person, beyond your tall, mounding, and trailing choices you will probably need additional mounding items to fill in the empty spaces of your container and, depending on the size of the pot, perhaps one or two more trailers.

size does matter

The next item to keep in mind is the size of your container, both width and height. If you are using one that is only 12 inches tall you do not want to put a plant in the container that will grow to be 48 inches tall, as there may be complications with the plant being top heavy and easily knocked over. Besides the practical aspects, the proportions will look off if the planting is too tall for the container. On the other hand, filling a large, 24-inch-wide and 3-foot-tall container with all impatiens is not wrong, but it is not very exciting either. For the best look, keep the maximum height of the plant at one-third to two-thirds the height of your container. This will provide you with a perfectly proportional look and one that will not be a safety hazard.

Always check the information on the back of the plant tag to determine height and spread. A container filled with the tall *Pennisetum glaucum* 'Purple Majesty', along with gazania for the mounding variety and *Dichondra* 'Silver Falls' for the trailer will leave you feeling a little flat. Besides the gazania remaining closed until the sun wakes it up, it does not have enough height to it. Replace the gazania with a more mounding plant and you will be happier with the look of your finished product. If you really like the look of gazania and really want to include it, then look for another upright variety that falls somewhere between the height of the ornamental millet and the gazania. Cut the number of gazanias that you intended to buy in half and replace them with the taller item. A good selection to do this with would be zinnia, angelonia, coreopsis, or *Salvia* 'Mystic Spires'.

Be sure to determine how aggressive a plant is, so that you do not end up with a container garden filled with one variety because the others have been choked out. If you really like the look of an aggressor, then plant the item, pot and all, into the container. This method keeps the aggressive plant in its place, and you will be able to continue to enjoy the look of all the components of your combo throughout the summer. Examples of large, aggressive plants are: *Ipomoea* spp., *Begonia* 'Dragon Wing', *Plectranthus* 'Silver Shield', and *Petunia* 'Tidal Wave'. These plants require very little care and reach amazing sizes by the end of the summer. Green thumb or not, you really cannot go wrong with these varieties.

Some plants do very well in the cool days and nights of spring, while others thrive in the heat of summer. Be aware that certain varieties planted in the spring may not provide color as you approach the warmer days of summer. Pansies, nemesia, and diascia will stall out or dieback in the heat of the summer; some may return to bloom again in the fall when the weather turns cool again. If you plant these varieties in the spring, you will need to have other components ready to replace these cool-weather lovers when the temperature rises.

Besides plant tags, you can learn more about the plants you are interested in by talking to garden center employees, reading store handouts, or doing a little research at your local library. Many retailers

spring and summer selections

cool weather	warm weather
Viola 'Matrix' (pansy)	*Begonia* 'Dragon Wing'
Lobularia maritima 'Snow Crystals' (alyssum)	*Hibiscus* 'Luna'
Delphinium 'Guardian'	*Torenia* 'Clown'
	Abutilon 'Bella' (flowering maple)
Lobelia erinus 'Regatta'	
Antirrhinum 'Solstice' (snapdragon)	*Capsicum* 'Chilly Chili' (ornamental pepper)
Dianthus 'Corona Cherry Magic'	
Phlox '21st Century'	*Pentas* 'Butterfly'
	Angelonia 'Serena'
	Spilanthes oleracea 'Peek-a-Boo'
Aquilegia 'Swan'	
Bellis 'Bellisima'	*Coleus* 'Kong'
Diascia spp.	
Nemesia spp.	

even have Web sites that you can visit to acquire more information on your chosen plants. The more you learn about the plants you are planning to incorporate into your container, the fewer disappointments you will have in your results and the happier you will be with what you have created.

As you read through the following chapters of this book you will find a plan-o-gram with each combination to help make it easier to shop and plant or to just inspire and give you a starting place. There will be a picture of the finished container garden along with a listing of the plants used and an overhead diagram (plan-o-gram) showing you where to place your plants in the container. When followed closely, the plan-o-gram will produce a container that looks like the picture in the book. You may also find plan-o-grams listed on recipe cards in your garden center or in gardening magazine advertisements.

Each plant variety in the plan-o-gram is marked with a U (upright), M (mounding), or T (trailing). In addition, there is information on light requirements, any special watering or fertilizer needs, and the size of the container in the photograph. Use these recipes as a guideline because it may be difficult to find the exact varieties and/or container pictured in this book. You are an artist and if you use the recipe along with a bit of your own creativity, you will be delighted at what a beautiful container garden you can design. Just remember: upright (tall), mounding, and trailing.

color matters

Color is the crowning glory of your container garden. If you feel a bit uncomfortable selecting the colors that will complement one another or look great together, try using a color wheel as your guide.

You can use four color groupings as guidelines to create your color scheme:

Monochromatic color schemes use a shade and tone of one hue or color, along with varying shades of that same hue. An example of these colors would be red-orange, orange, and orange-yellow. These colors fall right next to one another on the color wheel.

Analogous schemes consist of colors that are adjacent to one another on the color wheel such as red, violet, and blue.

Complementary schemes use two hues that are on opposite sides of the color wheel, such as violet and yellow or blue and orange.

Polychromatic would be a combination of many different colors—your choice!

You can give your container garden a more cool, calming, and serene look by using purples, blues, and green versus one that is jazzy and spicy, incorporating the hot colors of red, orange, and yellow.

Color can also come from the leaves of your plants. There are many shades of green, from the beautiful green of *Dichondra* 'Emerald Falls' to the bright chartreuse green of *Ipomoea* 'Marguerite'. In addition, many accent varieties have variegated leaves that add yellow and white to the various shades of green, like vinca and ivy. Other colors that serve as good accents are purple (e.g., *Strobilanthes dyerianus* or Persian shield, and *Iresine* 'Purple Lady') and silver (e.g., *Dichondra* 'Silver Falls' and *Plectranthus* 'Nicolleta').

intriguing texture

Color is not the only feature that can attract attention in your container garden. The texture of the leaves and flowers can create yet another dimension to your container and add a lot of excitement. Keep an eye out for different shapes, different shades, and different textures in the leaves as well as unusually shaped flower petals as you shop for plants. Put the plants together in your shopping basket or directly into the container that you have selected and look for similarities and differences. The large leaves of a *Begonia* 'Dragon Wing' combined with the smaller, jagged leaves of a *Verbena* 'Aztec' give interest and contrast. Furry or shiny leaves, like *Stachys* 'Fuzzy Wuzzy' or *Plectranthus* 'Silver Shield', can do the same as well and

This window box could use a little help with texture and color to change it from a weedy look to one that will allow your eye to relax and enjoy.

even beg the onlooker to touch. Since the petals of a petunia are the same as calibrachoa, putting these two selections together would not capture the eye as much as putting that same calibrachoa together with *Perilla* 'Magilla' and geraniums.

There are times that your flowers may take a rest, leaving only the leaves as the star of the show. Having different textures to look at will add to your container garden . . . like a second showing that can be just as beautiful as the first. Try adding plants such as ferns, hostas, or an artichoke to add variety. If each is different and unique, then there will be added interest and the viewing pleasure increases.

accent plants

Many wonderful selections—more than the typical ivy that has graced containers for years—add accents and even color without blooms to your container. These accents are available in all three categories (i.e., tall, mounding, and trailing), and you'll see many examples of these wonderful plants as you read through this book.

Whether incorporating the tall *Perilla* 'Magilla' with its tricolor leaves or the trailing, futuristic look of *Dichondra* 'Silver Falls', accent plants for container gardening have never been more fun or more colorful. The vivid, mounding colors of *Coleus* 'Kong' or the dark, trailing beauty of *Iresine* 'Purple Lady' are additional examples of accent plants that can add wonderful color to your container garden.

Another interesting alternative is to add indoor houseplants to your container gardens. It can be fun to incorporate these unique shapes, colors, and textures to your combinations and then be able to bring them indoors for the winter as an added bonus. These plants are not always readily found in the outdoor garden center due to their tenderness in colder zones, but you may find them just inside the outdoor garden center door. So be sure to take a peek inside the "Houseplants" or "Indoor Tropical" section of your garden center.

accent plants

- *Capsicum* 'Black Pearl' (ornamental pepper)
- *Iresine* 'Blazin' Rose'
- *Coleus* 'Kong'
- *Alternanthera* 'Purple Knight'
- *Dichondra* 'Emerald Falls'
- *Dichondra* 'Silver Falls'
- *Pennisetum glaucum* (ornamental millet)
- *Spilanthes* 'Peek-a-Boo'
- *Plectranthus* 'Silver Shield'
- *Isolepsis* 'Live Wire'
- *Strobilanthes dyerianus* (Persian shield)
- *Perilla* 'Magilla'
- *Helichrysum petiolare* (licorice plant)
- *Coleus* 'Aurora'

You will be amazed at the unusual and stunning combinations you can create when you no longer imprison these beauties indoors.

Tropicals are also a fun category that many gardeners have not had the chance to enjoy outdoors. But when you add a large, tropical selection to a large container, you will get the attention of friends and neighbors wanting to see just what you have done. Some do require sun, like the *Musa* spp. (banana tree), but there are tropical varieties that with a little tender loving care, such as heavy mulching, will winter over in cooler climates of the country. Better yet, make your own indoor container garden by gathering all the tropical plants that you used in your outdoor container gardens this summer and combining them to extend the life and enjoyment of these plants. Who knows, you may even be able to use them again next year!

Want to go all out? Why not try a carpet rose (*Rosa* 'Flower Carpet') for an interesting, very Victorian look to your container garden? You will need to wear gloves when planting and tending to these container plants because of their thorns. In the fall, you can then transplant the rose bush to your garden bed. Although most roses are quite particular and may not make it through all this planting and replanting, carpet roses are a bit more forgiving.

Many stores are now stocking small succulents in the houseplant section of the garden center. These unique-looking plants add interest to a stone container or any shallow receptacle. They require very little water and will look great both indoors and out. You can create a miniature storybook land by adding walkways, using tiny pebbles or marbles, a garden wall with broken tops of terra-cotta pots and ceramic pieces that would normally be used in a fish tank. Add succulents all around these hard-good additions and even sedges or small grasses for some height. Succulent gardens are one of the latest trends in gardening.

Dwarf conifers are also a big trend in Europe, and they're starting to take root in the States as well. As with succulents, you can enjoy a container garden filled with dwarf conifers all year round by bringing it indoors during the colder months of winter.

Still having a difficult time getting started? Try picking one item that you would really like to have in your container and work around that plant or start with the upright variety of your choice. By selecting the upright first you will know just how much space is left and how many mounding and trailing varieties you will need to fill that space. Remember: Your upright variety is usually the star of the show, so make sure it is one that you'll be happy looking at for the rest of the season.

plant placement

Once you have selected the plants for your container garden, you will need to think about how you would like your finished product to look. This is where your plan-o-gram can refresh your memory and help with the placement of the plants.

Basic container design calls for tall or upright plants to be placed in the middle with the mounding and trailing plants gathered around it. Although this placement is beautiful and elegant, your container gardens do not have to conform to this general format. The tiered effect with heights graduated from upright in the back to trailing in the front is very popular. This works very well when you are planning to place your finished container garden against a wall or in a corner. With this setup you are able to see all the plants without having to move the container around. In addition, each plant in the container will get an ample amount of light since the taller plant in the back will not be shading the smaller plants.

planting

You made your list, filled out the plan-o-gram, shopped, and purchased everything you will need to prepare your container garden. Now it's time to assemble your work of art.

Place newspaper down around the area that you will be planting to catch any spilled container mix and facilitate clean up. After you have checked for drainage holes and cracks, place a coffee filter inside the bottom of the container to cover up the drainage hole. Although this is not required, it will keep the container mix from escaping through the hole and will slightly hasten the water's escape. Fill your container up to 1 to 2 inches below the lip of the pot with container mix. It is important that you do not overfill the container. You do not want the mix flying all over the place while you are planting or water and mix running out over the lip during watering and rain showers. You can always add container mix as needed.

Next, read the directions and work in the appropriate amount of slow-release fertilizer into the soil for the size container you are using. This is also be a good time to add water retention crystals. If you choose to use the liquid fertilizer, you can apply this after your container garden is complete.

Do a final check on the plant placement by putting your potted plants directly on top of the container mix. This will give you final confirmation that you are ready to plant or will provide the opportunity to move the plants around to find the perfect placement. It is a lot easier to change your mind now than after everything is planted.

When you are satisfied with the look of the combination, it is time to plant. If you use slightly moist potting mix, it will be easier to work with and there will be less dust. Press down gently on the mix to prevent your plants from sinking as the soil settles over time. (If your plants do sink, do not add more soilless mix to try to build the container volume back up because you may suffocate some of your plants.) If this happens, your only choice is to remove the plants, add more of the container mix, and plant again.

Begin by digging a hole in the mix either with your trowel or hand. When preparing the hole, give yourself a little extra room on all sides and on the bottom. If you are not sure if the hole is deep enough or wide enough, simply place the plant—pot and all—into the hole and you will instantly see if more digging is required.

Release plants from their pot by tapping or squeezing the sides of the container and support the plant with your hand at the soil line as you tip the pot over. Your plant should easily break free from the pot and fall into your hand. If not, try tapping on the pot a little harder. Never try to pull the plant out of the pot by the stem; you could easily break the top of the plant from its base and be left with nothing or cause the plant severe damage. Some containers even have a release button on the bottom that looks like a bubble. When you are ready to remove the plant from one of these containers, simply push up on the button and the plant will loosen just enough to allow easy removal. If there are roots growing out of the bottom of the pot, it usually means that the plant is root bound and may take a bit of coaxing and patience to get it out of its pot. A plant becomes root bound when it is held for too long at the grower or garden center and it is anxiously waiting someone to come along and plant it into a bigger container. This doesn't mean that it is a bad plant unless it

has started to physically deteriorate. If the plant is root bound but still appears to be in good health, then simply snip off the roots that are growing outside of the pot and you will be able to easily release it from the container when you are ready to plant. Don't worry! You are not damaging the plant by doing this.

Once you have removed the plant from its pot, it is good to loosen up the roots. This will help to break up the mass and give the roots a sense of freedom. Spread the roots in the hole you have dug, fill with your soilless mix, press gently, and water.

Have you ever taken a plant out of a pot only to find an endless circle of roots? As the plant was growing and the roots hit the wall of the inside of the pot, they had nowhere else to go so they took a right or a left turn and just kept on growing in circles. This is called being root bound (see photo on right). This loop must be broken or the plant could eventually strangle itself. Before you plant, use your trowel to cut some of the roots on each side. Then, gently separate and massage the roots and spread them out in the hole you have dug. Finally, plant as usual and your plant should do just fine.

For those plants not requiring preparation before planting, just place the plant in the hole that you have dug and fill all around with your container mix, checking to make sure that the soil line in the container is not any higher or lower than the original soil line of the plant in the pot. Do the same for each plant. If you find that your last plant is bigger than the remaining space, just loosen the dirt around the plant's roots and gently slide the plant into the hole, spreading the roots apart, and then cover them with dirt. Remember to gently

Using a combination of variegated ivy, impatiens, and cyclamen in hanging grass or moss half-baskets, you can brighten up a shady wall.

press the soil down around each plant's base when you are done planting to remove any pockets of air. This prevents water from pooling in one area while the other areas receive only runoff. Add soil where needed to even out the level in the entire container and give the container a good watering.

If you pull the plant from its pot and the dirt falls off to expose the roots, do not panic. Just gently spread the roots in the hole you have created and cover them with your container mix as soon as possible. The longer you wait to cover the roots with soil, the greater the chance that you could cause severe damage to the root system. You can mix in some of the original soil that fell off of the rootball in your soil to provide the roots with a familiar surrounding.

If you are preparing a hanging basket and the bottom of the container is round, simply place it on top of an empty container to keep it stable until you have finished planting. If you are using a wire basket and there is nothing in the bottom of the grass/coco liner to capture and hold a small reservoir of water, you can place a pie tin in the bottom and accomplish virtually the same results.

When planting your hanging basket, you will need to be careful of any items that have height. Smaller hanging baskets will look over-grown quickly if a tall plant is added to the mix. Instead, stick primarily with mounding and trailing varieties unless the upright is shorter than most, such as *Pelargonium* x *hortorum* 'Showcase' (zonal geranium), or you have a very large basket that can handle an upright plant.

Grass baskets can be planted just on the top (in the soil), or, for a really full look, make a few slits in the coco basket with a pair of scissors and into each slit gently push the soil and roots of a plant. Add soilless mix to cover and fill the basket until it is about two-thirds full. Plant the top and fill the rest of the basket with mix, taking time to gently press down the soilless mix all around the base of the plants. Water thoroughly.

If you are using loose grass or sphagnum from a bag, then line the bottom of the wire basket and slide the plants you would like to use gently through the wire wall of the basket, resting the rootball or soil with the roots on the grass. Continue to build the grass walls, securing the side plantings, and fill with soil to hold everything in place. Finish planting the top of the basket and water thoroughly.

water, fertilize, deadhead

Keep a close watch on the watering needs of your container gardens since you are their only source of a refreshing drink, with the exception of rain. Watering in the morning is best. The plants will be able to quench their thirst through the warmest parts of the day and will avoid the danger of diseases that can develop from wet foliage during the cooler temperatures of the night. You will also want to fertilize routinely to keep the plants healthy and strong. Plants in containers do not have access to nutrients other than the ones you provide.

Many but not all varieties need to be deadheaded to tell the plant you are interested in having more flowers appear. This process is simple and can be done at the same time that you water your plants. When you see a bloom just beginning to fade, use your thumb and finger to pinch off the flower. Avoid letting the blooms go to seed and you will continue to enjoy beautiful color from your annuals all season long. For plants that do not need to be deadheaded, an occasional cleanup will keep your container garden looking fresh and attractive.

a quick checklist of the container gardening process

items needed

✔ Gloves
✔ Plan-o-gram
✔ Container
✔ Soilless mix
✔ Fertilizer

✔ Trowel/hand shovel
✔ Plants
✔ Water
✔ Newspaper or drop cloth

at the store

✔ Take your plan-o-gram to the store.
✔ Select your container with a hole for drainage.
✔ Grab one or two bags of container mix (depending on the size of your container).
✔ Pick an all-purpose fertilizer.
✔ Select your plants.
✔ Perhaps purchase an accent piece or artistic item to dress up your container.

at home

✔ Fill the container up to 1 to 2 inches from the top with the soilless mix.
✔ Add fertilizer according to the package directions and mix into the soil.
✔ Position plants before planting.
✔ Dig the holes and plant each until the container is complete.
✔ Press soil gently and add container mix to even out the soil level.
✔ Water thoroughly.
✔ Water and deadhead routinely.
✔ Enjoy!

coping with nature and insects

Two forces, nature and insects, do not always cooperate with gardeners. Each year will bring new challenges. Why? Because just like snowflakes, no two springs, summers, or autumns are exactly alike.

nature

As a gardener, you need to be realistic. The chance of something in your container garden not doing well is pretty good. Either the summer was too hot or too dry, or the spring too cool or too wet. Each year you can count on the weather being different than the year before, and more often than not it is anything but optimum. Each and every area of the country seems to suffer a weather blip, providing challenges to gardeners, especially container gardeners. Just because your hibiscus was the talk of the town last year doesn't mean that it is going to keep that same beauty this year.

When nature tests you, it is best to face the test head on. If temperatures are too hot, place the container garden in a cooler place and water more frequently. If the weather is too wet, find a temporary spot under the eaves of your home or even under a tree to protect your plants. If there is an unusually late spring or early autumn freeze, bring your containers indoors or cover them with a sheet until the next morning. If, for whatever reason, you lose a plant and find yourself with an empty hole in your container garden, fear not and look at this as a fun opportunity to add a new plant, a ceramic baby bird, or a stone garden angel. The empty space will be instantly filled and give a new look to your container.

insects

When it comes to bugs, you have four easy choices: Pick the infested leaf or stem off the plant and dispose of it, squash the bugs, apply an insect killer specific for what is ailing your plant, or just let whatever is eating away at the leaves have at it and hope that it will eventually have its fill and leave.

If you are going to grow your container garden outdoors, you are going to have more than just your neighbors enjoying them. If there is a particular plant that seems to be the favorite of your voracious friends, then the best solution to save you time, effort, and additional headaches is to carefully remove that plant and replace it with a totally different variety.

If you really cannot stand to look at the devastation that is being done to your prize dahlia or the holes in your hosta any longer, the first step to conquering your enemy is identifying it.

identification

If you can capture your hungry bug in a jar, drive it over to your local county cooperative extension office (look in the phone book for the closest one) for identification. This service is usually free, and you will be able to find out what you are battling and get suggestions on the best ways to rid yourself of that pest.

If you cannot capture the insect, bring a damaged leaf sample into the garden center, and the staff may be able to help. You may also want to purchase a magnifying glass and, along with a pest identification book or Web site, use it to help identify your targets.

Why would having a pest identified be worth your while? You should always take into consideration that the damage you are seeing may not even be from a bug. There are many insecticides to choose from, and you really want to select the right one to take care of the problem you are experiencing. Most insecticides are pretty effective; however, you must read the directions thoroughly before applying. Be careful with these chemicals, as they can be dangerous to your plant and to you. If your skin comes into contact with any pesticide, wash the affected area immediately.

contact pesticides

Insecticides, or pesticides, can be divided into two groups: contact or systemic. Contact pesticides require thorough application on the plant to cover the affected area. This may require more than one application to get the job done. Contact pesticides can be purchased in many different forms, such as powder, liquid, and granules, and some will require dilution. Read the label thoroughly to prevent damaging your plants. Wear the appropriate gloves and/or facemask if required by the label, and do not inhale the chemical fumes as

want a quick fix?

Fill a bucket with warm water and add a gentle dishwashing soap. Wipe down the top and bottom of each leaf and stem with the soap mixture. This will temporarily help to eliminate and/or reduce common insects, such as spider mites.

you are mixing. Remember that once you have mixed your pesticide with water, you must use it up completely. If you do not know what to do with any leftover pesticide, try sharing it with your neighbors or applying it to other garden plants. Always clean your spraying equipment, whether it's a hand pump or a hose-end sprayer, so that it will be ready for future applications. Other contact pesticides are sold ready to use, and there is no dilution required.

systemic pesticides

Systemic pesticides can be applied to the soil or leaves and is taken up by the plant, moving internally throughout its system. It takes longer than the contact pesticides to be effective but also last longer. This is a very easy and effective method to use with good results if the pest that you are after is listed on the insecticide.

insecticidal soap

Insecticidal soaps are a good choice for the environmentally conscious gardener. They are available at most garden centers and are made to kill the insect pests without adversely affecting the environment. Insecticidal soaps need to come in direct contact with the pests and should be applied either early in the morning or late in the evening to sustain the time that the soap remains wet. This is important since once the soap dries it is no longer effective. The soap works by washing away the protective outside coat on the body of the insect. This allows the soap to disrupt the normal cell membrane functions internally and eventually cause the insect to die. Insecticidal soaps work best on aphids, whiteflies, spider mites, and mealy bugs. Although safe for the environment, there are drawbacks to using insecticidal soaps, and multiple applications are necessary. Some plants, such as ferns and bleeding hearts, may be sensitive to soaps. These soaps can also be irritating to your skin and eyes. On the plus side, they are biodegradable, can be applied to food-bearing plants, and are friendly and non-toxic to the environment, people, birds, and animals. It is less likely that the pest will develop a resistance to the insecticidal soap.

beneficial bugs

Not all bugs are bad, though. Some, called beneficial insects, are natural predators or parasites of the bugs that are munching on your

don't bring the pests in

Considering bringing your plants indoor for the winter? Before bringing any plants indoors, check and spray for insects like spider mites or mealy bugs. You may also wash down the leaves with soapy water and remove any dead leaves that may be harboring other trouble. Your plants will look fresh and will be a beautiful addition to your indoor décor.

plants. Ladybugs, or ladybird beetles, are perhaps the best known of the beneficial insects. Ladybugs are cute and have voracious appetites, so most gardeners do not mind having them around. But what about the bigger and uglier insects? Spiders eat many of the insects that would love to sink their mandibles into your plants. The praying mantis, while big and scary looking, feasts upon grasshoppers, beetles, and other insects that cross their path. If you're not sure whether to save or sacrifice an insect in your garden, check with your local cooperative extension office, garden center, or master gardener, and be sure to choose chemicals that attack only the harmful insects in your garden and not the beneficial ones.

winter preparation

At the end of the season, when temperatures are beginning to freeze at night, you need to prepare your container for winter. It is best not to try to overwinter anything in your container, unless you are going to bring it indoors. A container is exposed to the elements on all sides, and unprotected plants reach temperatures much lower than if they were planted in a garden bed. These extreme temperatures can be damaging to their roots. This will weaken and eventually cause the plants to die, so either transplant the plants that you want to save for next year into a garden bed or bring them indoors for the winter.

Freezing soil and water can also damage your container. As discussed earlier, moisture in the potting mix will cause it to expand as it freezes, which can crack or push your decorative containers out of shape. To keep containers looking their best, clean them well and then store in the garage or basement.

putting it all together

Now that we've covered everything from selecting containers, matching plants, and planting and caring for your container gardens, you are ready to start having some fun. Use the combinations in the following chapters to fuel your creativity and inspire you to bring color and excitement to every area around your home.

starting simply 2

The following pages contain recipes for simple container gardens. When you are cooking and you follow the recipe, you are rewarded with a delicious meal. In this book, if you follow each recipe and plan-o-gram, you will be rewarded with a lovely, blooming creation.

If you are a one-color or one-variety type of gardener or are just looking for a nice container that requires the least amount of effort, then this chapter is for you.

There is nothing in the gardening books that says a container garden has to be a selection of different kinds of plants. Instead, you can go for the most basic of all container gardens by selecting one variety in one color or one variety in many colors. Sometimes referred to as a monoculture planting, this type of combination garden will save you time when you are shopping and you will not need a plan-o-gram. Instead, decide on the container that you will be using and determine how many plants you will need to purchase. Planting is a snap. In minutes you will have a beautiful container garden.

monoculture, one color

If you love red, you can make an easy red container by using all *Pelargonium* x *hortorum* 'Designer Red' (zonal geraniums). If purple is your favorite color, then how about *Angelonia* 'Serena' in purple or lavender? By showing off the delicate, orchid-like blooms, you will enjoy the soft colors along with the beauty of this annual and receive compliments from family and friends. Whatever your favorite color is, you can make a container garden in it to enjoy all summer long.

If you like the one color look but want to add some depth, then one trailing plant or tall plant in the same color is all it takes to add a bit of dimension to your monochromatic container. Place a trailer either directly in front or to the side or a tall plant in the middle or to the side for an attractive addition.

monoculture, mix

Perhaps you would like more than one color or shade of the same variety in your container garden. Many garden centers provide their customers with trays or flats of one variety in many colors. These mixes are very popular in Europe, and here in the States you can save yourself a lot of time by purchasing these mixes by the flat or pot. The color combinations are well matched, since they are mixed by the breeding companies and sold to growers with the right percentage of colors. Many of these mixes are even named by the breeding companies, making it easy for you to remember if you wish to buy it again. For example, the *Impatiens* 'Super Elfin Cha-Cha Mix' is a combination of warm-toned colors—ruby, scarlet, and salmon—with a touch of white. When you arrive in the garden center, rather than trying match colors that will go together yourself, grab flats of the color combinations you like, check out, and plant them in your containers.

two plants

Another basic container combination is one with two different kinds of plants. You can choose two varieties that both flower, or one flowering plant and one foliage accent, such as an ivy to trail over the edge of the container or a taller foliage or flowering plant to add height. Or you can try flowers in contrasting or complementary colors. This is a great exercise to warm up for the larger combinations in the following chapters.

When using two different varieties, I recommend one upright and one mounding variety, or one mounding and one trailing variety. Using an upright and a trailing plant will look like your container is missing something in the middle.

combination 1

a *Viola* 'Frosty Rain' (M) (pansy)

difficulty Easy

container 10-inch round terra cotta

light Sun

comments This combination is great for spring and fall and covers itself in blooms. Pansies and violas come in many different colors and color combinations. These smaller-petaled flowers bring plenty of color to your container and a smile to everyone's face. There are so many flowers you can hardly see the stems and leaves.

tip This container is small enough that you can move it to different locations around your house to freshen your deck or landscape. Plant a few in a smaller container to bring indoors to continue to enjoy.

combination 2

a *Impatiens* 'Fusion Glow' (U/M)

difficulty Easy

container 12-inch stone

light Part shade

comments Unique, tropical-looking flowers will add the bright color of yellow to your shade garden. This flower form is so stunning that it makes a strong statement all by itself, and there is no need to plant any other flowers in the same container. These plants will grow to about 12 inches tall.

tip Use a decorative chair to place the container on or nestle it in your garden in a place that needs a little color.

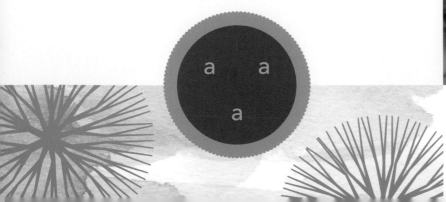

combination 3

a *Begonia richmondensis* (M)

difficulty Easy

container 14-inch, round, stone, short pedestal

light Shade

comments This is a hardy begonia that, given a shady location, will do quite well. If given protection, it can even be grown in a warm winter location.

tip Purchase the cute, ceramic mushrooms on a wooden base from most garden centers. They come in many sizes, shapes, and colors and add a touch of additional color and surprise for anyone passing by. They can be used year after year in either your container garden or garden bed. In the winter, store the ceramic mushrooms in a warm, dry, location to preserve them for many years.

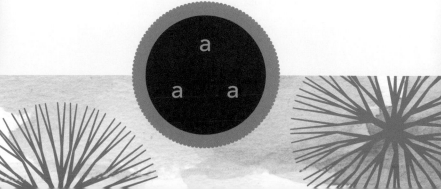

combination 4

a   *Helianthus* 'Ballad' (dwarf sunflower) (U)

difficulty Easy

container 16-by-6-inch, metal, rectangle

light Sun

comments This allergy-free, dwarf sunflower is perfect for containers or for a spot indoors; it loves the heat and grows to be 24 to 30 inches tall. You can plant the sunflowers or simply drop the pots directly into the rectangular container. If the tops of the pots are showing, cover them with a bit of sphagnum moss.

tip This container is great as a gift plant for anyone that needs a little sunshine in their day. You can't help but smile when you see these bright and cheerful flowers.

a   a   a   a

combination 5

a   *Primula* 'Primlet Lavender Shades' (M)

difficulty Easy

container 12-by-5-inch, rectangular ceramic

light Sun/Part sun

comments This scented primula features blooms that resemble mini-rose bouquets. It grows to a height of 5 to 6 inches and spreads to 5 to 7 inches. It makes for a great start to the gardening season, when you just have to have some live color in your home. 'Primlet' is available anytime from late winter to early spring and comes in eleven different colors.

tip This beautiful double-bloomed primula can be enjoyed indoors or out. A container of 'Primlet' in shades of red, rose, or pink makes for a beautiful Valentine's Day gift.

combination 6

a *Petunia* 'Easy Wave Rosy Dawn' (M/T)

difficulty Easy

container 16-inch, round, stone planter on pedestal

light Sun

comments This container garden looks elegant and dramatic when placed on a pillar, yet is incredibly easy to plant and maintain. This fast-growing petunia grows to a height of 6 to 12 inches, spreads 2½ to 3 feet, and blooms freely all season long with no need to cut it back. It performs well in the heat as well as in cooler conditions and is also available in blue, white, pink, and red. Fertilize routinely to continue the flush of blooms.

tip This petunia is suitable for hanging baskets, too.

combination 7

a *Impatiens* 'Super Elfin Splish Splash Mix' (M)

difficulty Easy

container 14-inch, round, grass-lined wire basket

light Shade

comments This impatiens mix grows to a height of 8 to 10 inches and spreads 12 to 14 inches. This is the first of several attractive mixes that you will see in this book.

tip Purchasing already-coordinated mixes at your garden center will make your hanging basket look like a designer created it. The 'Splish Splash' mix combines three complementary colors that look beautiful together. When you plant your container, don't worry about using a plan-o-gram to determine color placement. They will automatically blend together beautifully.

combination 8

a   *Capsicum* 'Medusa' (ornamental pepper) (U)

difficulty Easy

container 8-inch, round, glazed ceramic

light Sun

comments This child-safe, ornamental pepper plant ranges from 6 to 8 inches tall and spreads from 4 to 6 inches. It loves the heat of the summer, but also performs well in the autumn—both indoors and out. The peppers are nonpoisonous but are not recommended for eating. The plant's colorful, 2- to 2½-inch fruit starts out ivory in color then changes from yellow to orange to bright red as it matures. A single plant can produce forty to fifty fruits, displaying the full range of colors at the same time.

tip This is a fast, easy, and colorful decoration for a Mexican fiesta dinner or for fall decorating.

a   a   a

a

combination

a *Tagetes* 'Durango Outback Mix' (marigold) (U/M)

difficulty Easy

container 12-inch, short, ceramic bowl

light Sun

comments These marigolds will grow to be 10 to 12 inches tall and spread 6 to 8 inches. The mix provides 2- to 2½-inch blooms in a coordinated range of colors. To maintain, deadhead the spent blooms for continuous color.

tip This mix is excellent as a summer-through-autumn combination.

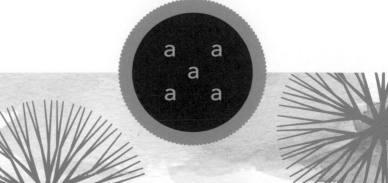

combination 10

a *Verbena* 'Quartz Polka Dot Mix' (M)

difficulty Easy

container 10-inch, round, plastic, terra-cotta color bowl

light Sun

comments This drought-tolerant verbena grows to a height of 10 to 12 inches and a spread of 12 to 14 inches. It performs well in the heat of the summer and will also tolerate a light frost. It performs well in hanging baskets too.

tip Another great verbena mix to try is the 'Quartz Waterfall Mix' that combines lavender, blue, white, and purple with a white eye.

combination 11

a *Viola* 'Panola Yellow' (pansy) (M)

b *Viola* 'Panola White' (pansy) (M)

c *Viola* 'Panola Fire' (pansy) (M)

difficulty Easy

container 14-inch, round, glazed ceramic

light Sun

comments These mounding plants grow to a height of 6 to 8 inches and a spread of 8 to 10 inches. The medium-sized pansies create a lot of color throughout the season and are particularly suited for autumn. The glazed-ceramic container used here complements the colors of the flowers well.

tip Place near your front door to welcome autumn visitors with a burst of color.

combination 12

a *Petunia* 'Dreams Neon Rose' (M) [pictured front right in a 12-inch pot]

b *Petunia* 'Dreams Burgundy' (M) [pictured front left in an 8-inch pot]

c *Petunia* 'Dreams Midnight' (M) [pictured back in a 14-inch pot]

difficulty Easy

container 8-, 12-, and 14-inch, round, terra-cotta pots

light Sun

comments These petunias reach heights from 10 to 15 inches and spread from 10 to 12 inches. The three different terra-cotta container styles that are shown here work in harmony with the rich colors of the petunias.

tip Planting one variety in each pot allows you to cluster or separate the three pots and reduces competition with other varieties.

combination 13

a *Angelonia* 'Serena Mix' (U) [pictured front left in a 12-inch container on a short pedestal]

b *Nemesia* 'Poetry Mix' (U) [pictured front right in a 10-inch container]

c *Diascia* 'Diamonte Mix' (M) [pictured back in a 12-inch container]

difficulty Easy

container 10- and 12-inch, round, stone containers on pedestals

light Sun

comments An easy yet elegant look is achieved by selecting a mix of three different varieties and putting each in its own container.

tip The nemesia will thrive in the cooler months and can be replaced by another variety when the summer months heat up.

combination 14

a *Hydrangea* 'Endless Summer' (U)
b *Petunia* 'Double Wave White' (T)

difficulty Easy

container 14-inch, square, tall, ribbed ceramic

light Part shade

comments This hydrangea is hardy to Zone 4 and will grow from 3 to 5 feet tall. The petunia will trail beautifully over the sides. Removing old flowers will encourage new blooms.

tip The petunias could be replaced by *Dichondra* 'Silver Falls' (T) in this combination. As autumn approaches or blooms begin to fade, plant the hydrangea in your garden bed to enjoy again next year.

combination 15

a *Impatiens hawkeri* 'Celebrette Purple' (New Guinea impatiens) (M)

b *Nephrolepis exaltata* (Boston fern) (U)

difficulty Easy   **light** Shade

container 12-inch, round, coco-lined wire basket with handle

type Mounding and upright

comments This lovely combination is easy to lift and relocate anywhere in the garden. It can be used as a hanging basket or brought indoors to enjoy throughout the winter. If brought indoors, you'll need to drop the basket into another container or put it on a large enough saucer to keep water from running onto your floor.

tip Substitute 'Celebrette Purple' with any of the 'Celebration' or 'Celebrette' colors. They will all work well in the coco-lined wire basket with the fern as your backdrop. Match the color of the New Guinea impatiens to the fabric on your patio cushions.

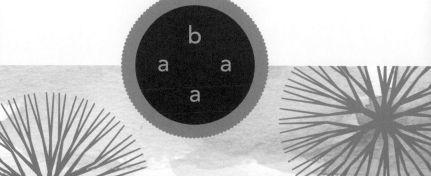

combination 16

a *Viola* 'Matrix Blue Frost' (pansy) (M)

b *Dianthus* 'Ideal White' (U/M)

difficulty Easy

container 12-inch lightweight fiberglass

light Sun

comments This combination will do very well in the cooler temperatures of spring. The dianthus grows from 8 to 10 inches tall and is heat and frost resistant. The pansies reach heights of 6 to 8 inches and have very large flowers. The 'Matrix' pansy variety is available in fifteen colors and six mixes.

tip Substitute the dianthus with *Lobularia maritima* 'Snow Crystals' (alyssum) or *Lobelia* 'Regatta White'.

combination 17

a *Abutilon* 'Bella Mix' (flowering maple) (U/M)

b *Hedera* 'Thorndale' (English ivy) (T)

difficulty Easy

container Any type of wicker basket

light Part sun/part shade

comments To create this container garden, first place a bicycle that is no longer being used—or one that you have picked up at a garage sale or flea market—in your garden bed. Attach the wicker basket already filled with planting mix to the bicycle and fill with abutilon and English ivy plants. This abutilon is also available in shades of apricot, pink, and red.

tip If you are trying to match a certain color scheme, spray paint the bicycle to match.

baaab

easy as 1-2-3 3

A-B-C or 1-2-3—that's how easy it will be for you to assemble the container gardens in this chapter. The combinations maintain the simplicity of the basic containers in chapter 2 while shaking it up a bit. These recipes incorporate three different varieties and apply the upright, mounding, and trailing concept. This is also where the plan-o-grams become important.

In this chapter there will be no more than three varieties to select and three varieties to plant. If you decide that you would like a larger container than what is called for in the recipe, double the items and plant each variety together. Better yet, mix it up.

Plant them together or alternate with the other two varieties you have selected. You can also cluster three or more containers planted in the same way together. Either way you can still be assured of a great finished look.

If you haven't begun to include your children in your home's container gardens, this would be a great time to start. Young children will be able to plant the single-plant containers, but older children and teens will love the creativity allowed by using three plants. If you let them select the plants and choose their placement, you will all have fun and your kids will feel ownership of the pots.

To help the process along, I group the plants that I bring home into three categories: upright, mounding, and trailing, and I let my son pick his favorite from each group to plant. It doesn't take a lot of time on their part (so they won't get bored or overwhelmed), and you expose them to what could turn into a lifelong hobby. Throughout the summer, as we use our deck for entertaining, dining, or just relaxing and enjoying an afternoon, it's fun to watch their container grow and thrive.

combination 18

a *Coleus* 'Lava Rose' (M/T)

b *Angelonia* 'Angelmist White Cloud' (U)

c *Pelargonium* × *hortorum* 'Designer Bright Red Improved' (zonal geranium) (U)

difficulty Easy

container 12-inch, raised, square terra-cotta

light Sun

comments This coleus really loves the sun but will also do well in the shade. The delicate orchid-like flowers of the angelonia will tower over the entire arrangement and call to onlookers to take a closer look. It will grow up to 14 inches in height.

tip The 'Designer' series comes in many shades of red. If you are unable to find 'Designer Bright Red Improved', then 'Scarlet', 'Salmon Red', or 'Violet' would be good substitutions.

combination 19

a *Dahlia* 'Melody Lisa' (U)

b *Perilla* 'Magilla' (U)

c *Plectranthus* 'Nicodemus' (T)

difficulty Easy

container 14-inch, round, fiberglass

light Sun

comments The dahlia will provide you with large blooms that can also be used as cut flowers, while the plectranthus will provide fragrance to this combination. The brilliant color of the perilla will take the lead when the dahlia is not in bloom.

tip Substitute *Dahlia* 'Melody Gypsy' for 'Melody Lisa'.

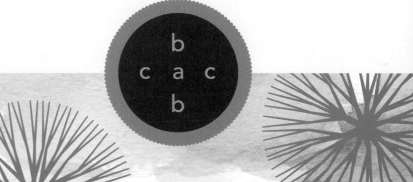

b
c a c
b

combination 20

a *Pelargonium peltatum* 'Colorcade Red' (ivy geranium) (U)

b *Lobelia* 'Temptation Dark Blue' (M)

c *Gaillardia* 'Torch Flame Red' (U)

difficulty Easy   **light** Sun

container 12-inch, terra-cotta bowl

comments This is a heat-tolerant combination and looks great on a patio table. The ivy geranium is very free flowering with dark green foliage that adds a striking contrast to the red flowers. Be sure to deadhead the geraniums as they start to fade; this signals the plant to continue flowering.

tip *P. peltatum* 'Colorcade Ruby', 'Burgundy', and 'Cherry Red' are also good color matches. For a little accent color in your lobelia, use *Lobelia* 'Periwinkle Blue'. It has a touch of white on each tiny flower and is very heat tolerant. If the lobelia begins to fade, remove it and add 'Chilly Chili' ornamental pepper, *Petunia* 'Easy Wave Purple' or 'Aztec Grape Magic'.

combination 21

a *Scutellaria* 'Veranda' (M/T)

b *Coleus* 'Kong Scarlet' (M)

c *Impatiens* 'Fanfare Orange' (spreading impatiens) (M/T)

difficulty Easy

container 12-inch, round terra cotta

light Shade

comments The orange and purple make great contrasting colors in this combination and are perfect for the summer and autumn. Scutellaria loves the heat and adds a beautiful touch of blue to your shade container or hanging basket. Even without flowers, the coleus is the star of the show in this mixed container.

tip Not crazy about orange? Then try *Impatiens* 'Fanfare Fuchsia' or 'Fanfare Pink Sparkle'.

combination 22

a *Coleus* 'Aurora Raspberry' (M)

b *Asparagus setaceus* (plumosa fern) (M)

c *Diascia* 'Whisper Cranberry Red' (M)

difficulty Easy

container 12-inch, round terra cotta

light Sun/Part sun

comments The coleus provides an abundant amount of color with practically no maintenance all season long. The fern adds a soft, wispy texture.

tip Substitute *A. setaceus* with *Isolepsis* 'Live Wire' or *A. densiflorus* 'Sprengerii' or 'Myersii'. Also try *Diascia* 'Whisper Dark Coral' instead of 'Whisper Cranberry Red' for a slightly different color combination.

combination 23

a *Pennisetum glaucum* 'Purple Majesty' (ornamental millet) (U)

b *Trachelium* 'Devotion Blue' (U)

c *Iresine* 'Purple Lady' (T)

[Also pictured in back: *Impatiens* 'Java Lilac Flame' (M)]

difficulty Easy

container 12-inch, round fiberglass

light Sun

comments Using unusual plants such as trachelium will keep your friends and neighbors coming back for more. *Trachelium* 'Devotion' also comes in white, burgundy, and purple.

tip 'Purple Majesty' can grow up to 4 to 5 feet tall. If you would like to use a more compact variety of ornamental millet, try 'Jester' (3 to 4 feet tall) or 'Purple Baron' (2½ to 3½ feet tall).

combination 24

a *Hibiscus* 'Luna Red' (U)

b *Petunia* 'Easy Wave White' (M/T)

c *Iresine* 'Purple Lady' (T)

difficulty Easy

container 14-inch, round fiberglass

light Sun

comments *Hibiscus* 'Luna' is a perennial hardy to Zone 5 and loves the heat. Its flower size will range from 6 to 8 inches across, and its habit is very bush-like. 'Luna' will provide you with many large, colorful blooms all summer long. *Petunia* 'Easy Wave' will mound 6 to 12 inches and spread 2½ to 3 feet, perfectly filling the open spaces of your container garden.

tip For a softer look, try *Hibiscus* 'Luna Pink Swirl' instead of 'Luna Red'. You may also substitute *Petunia* 'Easy Wave Shell Pink', 'Salmon', or 'Pink' for 'Easy Wave White'.

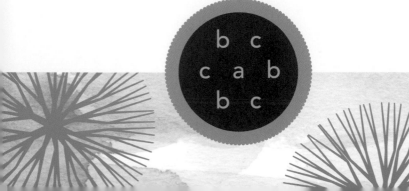

b   c
c a b
b   c

combination 25

a *Impatiens* 'Jungle Gold' (U)

b *Coleus* 'Wizard Velvet Red' (U)

c *Iresine* 'Purple Lady' (T)

difficulty Easy

container 14-inch, round clay

light Shade

comments The golden color of the impatiens and its orchid-like flowers will brighten any shady area. It will grow 15 to 18 inches tall and spread 12 to 14 inches. It is a big plant that loves hot weather. The delicate golden edge on the leaves of the coleus is a nice accent to the *Impatiens* 'Jungle Gold'.

combination 26

a *Petunia* 'Wave Pink' (M/T)

b *Petunia* 'Wave Purple' (M/T)

c *Pennisetum setaceum* (fountain grass) (U)

difficulty Moderate

container 36-by-18-inch, rectangular stone planter

light Sun

comments This container combination loves the hot weather and is virtually maintenance free. The petunias offer nonstop blooms, grow to be 4 to 6 inches tall, and spread 3 to 4 feet with absolutely no deadheading. The fountain grass is hardy in Zones 8 through 10.

tip Other 'Wave' colors that can be used are blue, misty lilac, lavender, or rose. Keep the 'Wave' petunias looking great with routine fertilization and trimming.

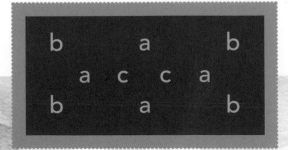

combination

a *Impatiens hawkeri* 'Celebration Light Salmon Improved' (New Guinea impatiens) (M)

b *Jamesbrittania hybrida* 'Bridal Bouquet' (bacopa) (T)

c *Dryopteris ludoviciana* (Southern fern) (U)

difficulty Easy

container 12-inch, terra-cotta-like plastic

light Part sun/part shade

comments Southern fern is perennial in Zones 4 through 10, grows to 18 inches in height, and spreads 12 to 18 inches. Other 'Celebration' colors that will work beautifully are 'Rose Star', 'Electric Pink', 'Orange', 'Pink', and 'Deep Red'.

tip You can also bring the Southern fern indoors to enjoy all winter long and use it again in your container gardens next spring.

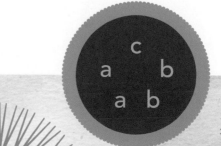

combination 28

a *Abutilon* 'Bella Pink' (flowering maple) (U/M)

b *Plectranthus* 'Silver Shield' (M/T)

c *Iresine* Purple Lady (T)

difficulty Easy   **light** Sun/part sun

container 12-by-12-inch, square terra-cotta

comments This is a great container garden for both spring and autumn that will also do well in hanging baskets. *Plectranthus* 'Silver Shield' can get aggressive, growing up to 30 inches, so either plant it in the pot that it comes in or use scissors to keep it under control. If you prefer, you can replace the *Plectranthus* 'Silver Shield' with *Plectranthus* 'Nicoletta', a much smaller variety. At the end of the season, the abutilon can come indoors.

tip For a height substitute, one of the abutilons can be replaced with *Pennisetum glaucum* 'Purple Baron', an ornamental grass. *Abutilon* 'Bella Yellow' or 'Bella Apricot Shades' can also be inserted for a different look.

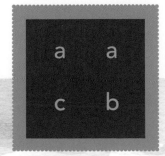

combination 29

a *Pentas* 'Butterfly Red' (U)

b *Hedera* 'Glacier' (English ivy) (T)

c *Plectranthus* 'Nicodemus' (T)

difficulty Easy

container 12-inch, round ceramic

light Sun

comments This container garden does well in the summer months and attracts butterflies and hummingbirds. If you cannot find variegated English ivy or *Plectranthus* 'Nicodemus', then replace it with an additional pentas or *Lamium* 'Jade Frost'.

tip Substitute a color mix of *Pentas* 'Butterfly Lavender Shades' and 'Butterfly Deep Rose' for 'Butterfly Red' for a softer appearance.

combination 30

a *Jamesbrittania hybrida* 'Breeze White' (bacopa) (U)

b *Verbena* 'Aztec Grape Magic' (T)

c *Pelargonium* x *hortorum* 'Designer Light Pink' (zonal geranium) (U/M)

difficulty Easy

container 14-inch, unglazed, stone pottery

light Sun

comments This is a beautiful container with loads of color that will look beautiful all summer long.

tip To add some variety, you can try a few other combinations, as well. Instead of *Verbena* 'Aztec Grape Magic', you can try *Verbena* 'Aztec Raspberry' or *Petunia* 'Suncatcher Deep Plum'. If you can't find the bacopa, *Angelonia* 'Angelmist White' makes a wonderful substitute. Deadhead the geraniums to keep the flush of color coming.

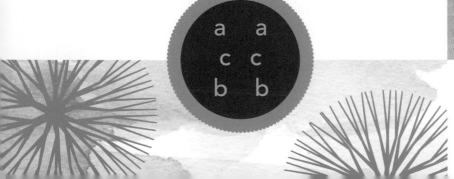

a a
c c
b b

combination 31

a *Impatiens hawkeri* 'Tango' (New Guinea impatiens) (M)

b *Spilanthes* 'Peek-a-Boo' (T)

c *Eragrostis* 'Wind Dancer' (U)

difficulty Easy

container 14-inch, round, lightweight stone-like fiberglass

light Sun/part sun

comments The unusual eye shape of the *Spilanthes* coupled with the orange color of the New Guinea impatiens make this a "spooktacular" combination for fall and Halloween. *Spilanthes* is also known as the toothache plant because it contains an analgesic that has been used to numb tooth pain.

tip Give the eragrostis a trim if it gets too wild.

combination 32

a *Calathea plowmanii* (U/M)

b *Impatiens hawkeri* 'Divine Mystic Mix' (New Guinea
impatiens) (M)

c *Isolepsis* 'Live Wire' (M)

difficulty Easy

container 14-inch, round, lightweight stone-like fiberglass

light Shade

comments Bring the calathea into the house for the winter
months to continue to enjoy the beautiful leaf pattern. *Isolepsis*
'Live Wire' adds great texture to this container and will grow
about 6 to 8 inches tall and spread 18 to 20 inches.

tip Try these New Guinea impatiens in orange, white, and
pink to add some variety, while still complementing the color
of the container.

c a
b b b
b c

combination 33

a *Carex* 'Gold Fountains' (sedge) (U)

b *Petunia* 'Suncatcher Coral Prism' (M/T)

c *Coleus* 'Florida Sun Jade' (U)

difficulty Easy

container 12-inch, round, stone pottery

light Part Sun

comments *Carex* 'Gold Fountains' is a perennial, hardy in Zones 5 through 9. It features narrow, green leaves with a gold border and will reach up to 10 inches in height and spread up to 20 inches. The carex in this container adds a different texture and brightens the overall container.

tip You can replace *Petunia* 'Suncatcher Coral Prism' with 'Suncatcher Dark Coral' for a more vibrant effect, as well as substitute *Coleus* 'Florida Sun Jade' with *Coleus* 'Florida Sun Splash', 'Alabama', 'Wizard Coral Sunrise', or 'Rustic Orange'.

combination 34

a *Isolepsis* 'Live Wire' (M)

b *Coleus* 'Wizard Rose' (U/M)

c *Zinnia* 'Zesty Lemon' (U)

difficulty Moderate

container 14-inch, round, glazed ceramic

light Sun

comments To give height to this container, add an antique decorative iron work or tree twigs that can be found at your local hobby and craft store.

tip Substitute *Zinnia* 'Zesty Pink' for 'Zesty Lemon'. Replace *Coleus* 'Wizard Rose' with 'Rustic Orange', 'Saturn', or 'Red Ruffles'.

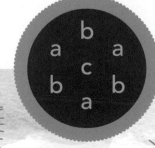

combination 35

a *Impatiens walleriana* 'Fiesta Apple Blossom' (double impatiens) (M)

b *Helichrysum* 'Licorice' (T)

c *Lobelia* 'Hot Arctic' (M/T)

d *Thelypteris* (maiden fern) (U)

e *Impatiens walleriana* 'Purple Pixie' (double impatiens) (M)

difficulty Easy

light Shade

container 12-, 10- and 6-inch, round, ceramic-glazed pots, clustered

comments Group all three containers together or place each in different parts of your deck and garden. The 6-inch pot will make a nice display on your patio table.

tip Substitute *Dichondra* 'Silver Falls' for the variegated helichrysum or *Impatiens* 'Pixie Double Sparkler Burgundy' for *I. walleriana* 'Purple Pixie'. Purchasing three of the same containers in different sizes will look very attractive clustered together or apart and will store easily inside one another.

combination 36

a *Petunia* 'Wave Misty Lilac' (T)

b *Plectranthus* 'Silver Shield' (M/T)

c *Pennisetum glaucum* 'Purple Majesty' (ornamental millet) (U)

difficulty Easy

container 14-inch, round, glazed ceramic

light Sun

comments Keep *Plectranthus* 'Silver Shield' in check with pinching or snipping.

tip Substitute *Petunia* 'Wave Misty Lilac' with 'Wave Pink', 'Wave Purple', or 'Wave Rose' for bolder colors. 'Wave Misty Lilac' and 'Silver Shield' are aggressive plants but play well together. This combination will be attractive even if you left out the ornamental millet.

combination 37

a *Chamaedorea elegans* (Neanthe Bella or parlor palm) (U)

b *Begonia* 'Dragon Wing Pink' (M)

c *Ipomoea* 'Marguerite' (ornamental sweet potato vine) (T)

difficulty Easy

container 18-inch, round, tall, glazed ceramic

light Shade

comments This is an enormous container that is heavy even empty. It is easiest to place the container where you want it to be first and then bring the container mix, fertilizer, and plants to it. Place empty plastic containers upside down in the bottom of this container to help reduce the amount of soilless mix you will need. The palm does well outdoors, but you should bring it inside when there is a chill in the air. Wipe down the leaves to reduce or eliminate the amount of pests it carries.

tip Substitute *Begonia* 'Dragon Wing Pink' with 'Dragon Wing Red'.

combination 38

a *Heuchera* 'Dolce Key Lime Pie' (M)

b *Capsicum* 'Black Pearl' (ornamental pepper) (U)

c *Verbena* 'Wild Fire Dark Red' (M/T)

difficulty Easy

container 8-inch, round, decorative, mixed terra-cotta

light Part sun/Part shade

comments *Heuchera* 'Dolce Key Lime Pie' is a perennial, hardy in Zones 5 through 11. The striking chartreuse leaves of the heuchera contrast brilliantly against the dark leaves of the ornamental pepper and the bright red of the verbena. If you would like more of the vibrant red in your combination, add another 'Wild Fire Dark Red' to the right side of the container between the heuchera and the 'Black Pearl' pepper.

a   b

c

combination 39

a *Rudbeckia* 'Irish Eyes' (black-eyed Susan) (U)

b *Coleus* 'Aurora Raspberry' (M)

c *Pelargonium* × *hortorum* 'Fantasia Violet Improved' (zonal geranium) (U)

difficulty Easy

container 8-inch, round, tall, cast stone

light Sun

comments The rudbeckia is a perennial, hardy in Zones 5 through 9. It will bloom July through September with bright yellow petals and an olive green eye. Its height reaches 24 to 36 inches. The coleus sports three different colors on each leaf, making it very versatile. It pulls together the colors of the rudbeckia and geranium perfectly.

tip You can substitute *Coleus* 'Aurora Black Cherry' for 'Aurora Raspberry'.

combination 40

a *Alocasia* 'Frydek' (U)

b *Porphyrocoma pohliana* 'Maracas Brazilian Fireworks' (M)

c *Impatiens walleriana* 'Fiesta Olé Purple' (double impatiens)
   (M)

difficulty Easy

container 6½-by-6½-inch square, glazed ceramic

light Part shade

comments The alocasia has dark, velvet-looking leaves
that can reach 2 to 3 feet in height. The real beauty of this
container is the bright purple, double blooms of the double
impatiens. When *P. pohliana* 'Maracas Brazilian Fireworks'
are done blooming, the green leaves with silver veins will add
an attractive accent.

tip When summer is over, bring *P. pohliana* 'Maracas Brazilian
Fireworks' indoors as a potted plant.

combination 41

a   *Thysanolaena* 'Maxima' (U)

b   *Pontederia* 'Singapore Pink' (U)

c   *Cyperus alternifolius* (umbrella plant) (U)

difficulty Easy

container 18-inch, round, plastic without drainage holes

light Full sun/part sun

comments This is a lovely water garden container. Water gardens are easy to create and maintain, and the foliage is unusual and very attractive. *Thysanolaena* 'Maxima' has bright green foliage and a bamboo look. *Pontederia* 'Singapore Pink' has dark green foliage and lavender-pink flowers. While *C. alternifolius* has an unusual umbrella-like look and will grow 3 to 4 feet tall.

tip Cover the base of the container with small rocks and keep the water to the level of the rocks at all times.

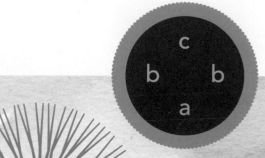

combination 42

a *Alocasia calodora* (Persian palm) (U)

b *Begonia rex* 'Fairy' (rex begonia) (M)

c *Impatiens* 'Fanfare Bright Coral' (M/T)

difficulty Easy

container 14-inch, square, tall ceramic

light Part sun/shade

comments *A. calodora* can grow up to 5 to 7 feet tall and is perfect for taller containers. If you cannot find *B. rex* 'Fairy', then pick any rex begonia that you like. 'Fanfare' has a mounding/spreading habit and is known for its heat tolerance.

tip You can change the color of this container garden by replacing *Impatiens* 'Fanfare Bright Coral' with 'Fanfare Fuchsia' or 'Fanfare Orchid'.

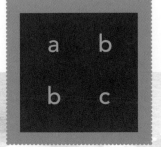

a b

b c

combination 43

a   *Kalanchoe* 'Flapjacks' (U)

b   *Kalanchoe* 'Donkey Ears' (U)

c   *Plectranthus* 'Skeeter Scatter' (M)

difficulty   Easy

container   14-inch, round, glazed ceramic

light   Sun

comments   *Kalanchoe* 'Flapjacks' is a popular succulent that originated in South Africa. The red color on the edge of the leaves adds a nice touch of color to this combination. *Kalanchoe* 'Donkey Ears' has long, waxy leaves that resemble donkey ears. Plantlets are produced on the edge of its leaves. If you wait for the roots to appear, you can gently break away the plantlets and place them on the soil surface to take root.

tip   Bring this container garden indoors and place it in a well-lit area and water very sparingly.

combination 44

a *Musa* 'High Color Mini' (dwarf banana) (U)

b *Begonia* 'Dragon Wing Red' (M/T)

c *Iresine* 'Purple Lady' (T)

difficulty Easy

container 14-inch, round, tall ceramic

light Sun

comments *Musa* 'High Color Mini' is a small, highly colored dwarf that will reach 2 to 4 feet in height. If you are unable to find it at your garden center, you can use *Pennisetum glaucum* 'Jester' or *Colocasia* 'Nancyana' as a substitute.

tip Substitute *Begonia* 'Dragon Wing Red' with 'Dragon Wing Pink' for a softer look.

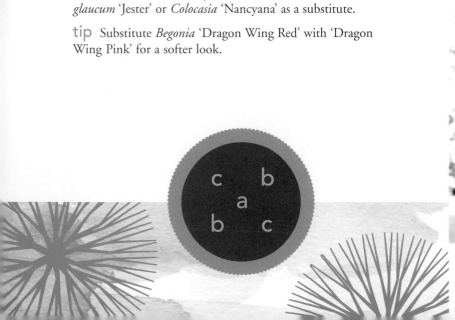

combination 45

a *Xanthosoma violaceum* (U)

b *Lamium* 'White Nancy' (T)

c *Alocasia portidora* (elephant ears) (U)

difficulty Difficult   light Shade

container 18-inch, round, tall ceramic

comments *Lamium* 'White Nancy' is a perennial, hardy in Zones 3 through 9. It is a fast-growing lamium variety and produces silver and green foliage with pure white flowers in early summer. It can spread up to 18 inches. *X. violaceum* will grow 4 to 6 feet tall with dark purple stems that really stand out. *A. portidora* has large, stunning, ruffled, upright leaves and can grow up to 6 feet tall.

tip If you would like to add more color, to this combo a large variety, such as *Begonia* 'Dragon Wing' or *Impatiens* 'Jungle Gold', would work well. For beautiful color from foliage at mid-range, add *Iresine* 'Blazin' Rose.'

combination 46

a *Cercis* 'Forest Pansy' (redbud) (U)

b *Sporobolus heterolepis* (prairie dropseed) (U)

c *Eucalyptus* 'Silver Drop' (U)

difficulty Moderate   **light** Sun

container 16-inch, round ceramic

comments *Cercis* 'Forest Pansy', hardy in Zones 5 through 9, is a deciduous tree producing rosy pink blooms in the spring, and in the autumn its leaves change to yellow. It has a mature height of 20 to 30 feet, so a container is not where you want this tree to remain. Prairie dropseed is a perennial, hardy in Zones 3 though 9. It features narrow, emerald-green leaves that turn a yellow to dark orange in autumn. It can reach 18 to 24 inches in height and in a garden bed will provide food and cover for wildlife.

tip *Cercis* 'Forest Pansy' does not transplant well as it matures, so it is best to get this plant into your garden bed as soon as possible in the fall.

combination 47

a *Impatiens walleriana* 'Fiesta Apple Blossom' (double impatiens) (M)

b *Sutera cordata* 'Abunda Giant White' (bacopa) (M/T)

c *Juncus patens* (common rush) (U)

difficulty Moderate

container 18-inch, round ceramic

light Part shade

comments No need to deadhead these impatiens; they will self-clean. This formal-looking container makes a beautiful accent for a backyard wedding.

tip A coco fiber basket with a flat base can also be used. Side plantings will enhance the look of the finished container.

fabulous four 4

Now that you are feeling comfortable and confident, perhaps you are ready be a bit more adventurous. By following the plan-o-grams in this chapter, you raise the look of your container gardens, as well as your expertise, another level. And you will do it all by using only four different varieties.

Chapter 4 will start to include larger grasses and tropical items, and containers will take on a different look and feel. There are combinations that are more subdued and some that start to incorporate a secondary upright item. As your containers get larger, just add an extra mounding, upright, or trailing item to fill any empty spaces. You can also use larger varieties that like to spread out, such as *Plectranthus* 'Silver Shield' or *Petunia* 'Tidal Wave'. When you have chosen the four varieties for your container garden, be sure to do a final check to make sure that they will all be happy living together. Check the light and water requirements and the size that you can expect the plant to grow. Remember to be careful of combining delicate plants such as lobelia with more aggressive items, such as *Begonia* 'Dragon Wing.'

Are you starting to feel like a designer? Many of the containers in this chapter start at 14 inches and go up in size. Do not be intimidated. If you incorporate the upright, mounding, and trailing design elements and refer to the color wheel to finish off the look that you desire, you are sure to be happy with the results.

combination 48

a *Begonia* 'Dragon Wing Pink' (U/M)

b *Coleus* 'Wizard Sunset' (M)

c *Dichondra* 'Silver Falls' (T)

d *Iresine* 'Purple Lady' (T)

difficulty Moderate

container 16-inch, lightweight fiberglass

light Sun/shade

comments This container combination is great for the heat. *Begonia* 'Dragon Wing' tends to be a very large, aggressive plant, since it can grow 12 to 15 inches tall and 15 to 18 inches wide—so plant it in your container in its original pot to keep it under control or it may overpower the iresine and coleus.

tip Substitute *Begonia* 'Dragon Wing Red' for 'Dragon Wing Pink' and *Coleus* 'Wizard Sunset' for 'Wizard Red Velvet' or 'Wizard Scarlet'.

c   b
d a a d
b   c

combination 49

a *Coleus* 'Wizard Jade' (U)

b *Veronica* 'Blue Bouquet' (U)

c *Nemesia* 'Sundrops Red' (M)

d *Lysimachia procumbens* 'Lyssi' (T)

difficulty Moderate

container 14-inch, etched terra-cotta

light Part sun

comments *Veronica* 'Blue Bouquet' is a perennial, hardy to Zone 5, and *L. procumbens* is a perennial, hardy in Zones 3 through 9. *Coleus* 'Wizard Jade' can grow 12 to 14 inches tall and 10 to 12 inches wide. Pictured in front are *Lisianthus* 'Forever Blue' and *Pelargonium peltatum* 'Summer Showers White Blush' (ivy geranium).

tip You can replace 'Lyssi' with *Calibrachoa* 'Starlette Yellow'.

combination 50

a *Leymus arenarius* (blue lyme grass) (U)

b *Coleus* 'Aurora Raspberry' (U)

c *Iresine* 'Purple Lady' (T)

d *Impatiens* 'Fusion Glow' (M)

difficulty Moderate

container 14-inch, round, glazed ceramic pedestal

light Shade

comments *L. arenarius* is a nice accent plant for both texture and its silvery blue color. A nice feature of *Impatiens* 'Fusion Glow' is its orchid-like flower form.

tip For a brighter look, replace *Coleus* 'Aurora Raspberry' with *Coleus* 'Wizard Mosaic' or *Artemesia* 'Silver Mound'. You can also try *Impatiens* 'Fusion Infrared' or 'Fusion Heat'.

b d
c a c
b d

combination 51

a *Begonia* 'Baby Wing Pink' (M)

b *Impatiens walleriana* 'Fiesta White' (double impatiens) (M)

c *Begonia rex* (M)

d *Caladium* 'Candidum Classic' (U)

difficulty Easy

container 14-inch, round, terra-cotta-like plastic

light Shade

comments The addition of the caladium gives a tropical feel, and the white leaves will brighten any shady area. Adding a little ornament like a butterfly on the rim of this pot can add an element of surprise to your garden.

tip This container can be brought indoors to enjoy throughout the winter.

combination 52

a *Impatiens walleriana* 'Fiesta Sparkler Rose'
(double impatiens) (M)

b *Ipomoea* 'Tricolor Pink Frost' (T)

c *Gaura* 'Siskyou Pink' (U)

d *Scaevola* 'Blue Fan' (T)

difficulty Easy   **light** Shade

container 18-inch, round, coco fiber/grass wire basket

comments *Guara* 'Siskyou' is a perennial, hardy in Zones
6 through 10.

tip Placing this container garden in a stand helps to give it
height really makes it stand out. The wire stand can be nestled
in a garden without disturbing the plants in the garden bed.
Water this container routinely. The grass basket will dry out
faster than a ceramic container.

combination 53

a *Iresine* 'Purple Lady' (T)

b *Begonia* 'Baby Wing Pink' (M/U)

c *Zantedeschia* 'Snow Cone' (calla lily) (U)

d *Petunia* 'Easy Wave Pink' (T)

difficulty Easy

container 14-inch, round fiberglass

light Part sun/part shade

comments The spotted leaves of the calla lily will provide interest even when it is not in bloom.

tip Substitute *Begonia* 'Baby Wing White' for *Begonia* 'Baby Wing Pink' or Petunia 'Easy Wave White' for 'Easy Wave Pink'.

d b
a c a
b d

combination 54

a *Porphyrocoma pohliana* 'Maracas Brazilian Fireworks' (M)

b *Dichondra* 'Silver Falls' (T)

c *Begonia* 'Baby Wing Pink' (M/U)

d *Impatiens hawkeri* 'Divine White' (New Guinea impatiens) (M)

difficulty Easy   **light** Shade

container 12-inch, round clay

comments When not in bloom, the leaves of *P. pohliana* 'Maracas Brazilian Fireworks' make a nice accent addition. It can be brought indoors to enjoy throughout the winter months. *Begonia* 'Baby Wing" will provide a soft pink color right through the heat of summer and will grow up to 15 inches tall and 12 inches wide.

tip For more color, replace *I. hawkeri* 'Divine White' with 'Divine Violet'.

combination 55

a *Dahlia* 'Melody Lisa' (U)

b *Petunia* 'Double Wave Pink' (T)

c *Senecio cineraria* 'Silverdust' (dusty miller) (M)

d *Strobilanthes dyerianus* (Persian shield) (U)

difficulty Moderate

container 14-inch terra cotta

light Sun

comments Deadhead the dahlia when blooms are fading. Persian shield can grow from 18 to 24 inches tall.

tip Substitute the dusty miller with *Catharanthus roseus* 'Titan Polka Dot' (vinca) for more flower power, or *Petunia* 'Double Wave Pink' with 'Double Wave White', 'Misty Lilac', 'Lavender', or 'Purple' for more color variety.

a
c d c
b b

combination 56

a *Begonia* 'Dragon Wing Red' (U/M)

b *Impatiens* 'Super Elfin Scarlet' (M)

c *Coleus* 'Wizard Jade' (U)

d *Coleus* 'Wizard Sunset' (U)

difficulty Easy

container 12-inch, terra-cotta-like plastic

light Shade

comments The hot colors of this container garden will look just as great at the end of summer as they do in the beginning. *Coleus* 'Wizard Jade' adds striking color contrast. Keep an eye on the begonia, as it can easily overtake the smaller items in your container garden.

tip *Coleus* 'Wizard Sunset' can be replaced with another *Coleus* 'Wizard Jade'.

a
c   d
b

combination 57

a *Abutilon* 'Bella Salmon' (flowering maple) (U)

b *Impatiens* 'Stardust Violet' (M)

c *Impatiens hawkeri* 'Celebrette Wild Plum' (New Guinea impatiens) (M)

d *Torenia* 'Clown Blue' (M)

difficulty Easy

container 12-inch, terra-cotta-like plastic

light Part sun/part shade

comments This container looks great even without the addition of a trailing plant. The torenia will grow to about 8 to 10 inches tall and 10 to 12 inches wide.

tip Substitute *Impatiens* 'Stardust Violet' with 'Coral Star' or 'Red Star', or replace *Torenia* 'Clown Blue' with 'Burgundy', 'Rose', or 'White Blush' for a different look.

combination 58

a *Abutilon* 'Bella Salmon Shades' (flowering maple) (U)

b *Impatiens* 'Stardust Salmon' (M)

c *Coleus* 'Wizard Velvet Red' (U)

d *Lysimachia* 'Goldilocks' (T)

difficulty Easy

container 12-inch, terra-cotta-like plastic

light Part shade/shade

comments This makes a great color combination for the late summer and into the fall. The bright chartreuse color of *Lysimachia* 'Goldilocks' adds a striking accent to the container.

combination 59

a *Petunia* 'Easy Wave Pink' (M/T)

b *Helichrysum* 'Licorice Lime' (T)

c *Anethum graveolens* 'Fernleaf' (dill) (U)

d *Plumbago* 'Escapade Blue' (U)

difficulty Easy   **light** Sun

container 12-inch, round, terra-cotta

comments This container does great in the hotter temperatures of the summer. *Plumbago* 'Escapade Blue' loves the heat and has a bushy-shrubby growth habit. Its height ranges from 12 to 18 inches and its spread is 18 to 24 inches.

tip If you are having a difficult time finding the dill, then look for *Salvia* 'Mystic Spires', *Perilla* 'Magilla' in purple or vanilla, or *Artemesia* 'Powis Castle' as suitable replacements. You can also substitute *Plumbago* 'Escapade Blue' with 'Escapade White'.

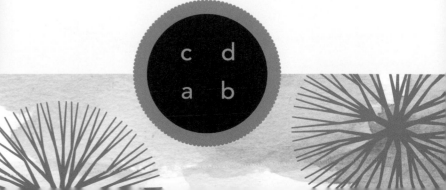

c   d

a   b

combination 60

a *Impatiens* 'Super Elfin Lipstick' (M)

b *Coleus* 'Black Dragon' (U)

c *Torenia* 'Clown Burgundy' (M)

d *Iresine* 'Purple Lady' (T)

difficulty   Easy

container   12-inch, round ceramic

light   Shade

comments   *Coleus* 'Black Dragon' can grow to be 12 to 14 inches tall, so it will make a nice backdrop for this container.

tip   If you would like a bit more height, try adding *Perilla* 'Magilla Purple' to the center. You can also substitute *Torenia* 'Clown White Blush' for 'Clown Burgundy' or *Impatiens* 'Super Elfin Lipstick' with 'Super Elfin Pink Swirl' or 'Stardust Rose'.

combination **61**

a *Coleus* 'Black Dragon' (U)

b *Iresine* 'Purple Lady' (T)

c *Dichondra* 'Silver Falls' (T)

d *Impatiens* 'Super Elfin Violet' (M)

difficulty Moderate

container 14-inch, round, glazed ceramic

light Shade

comments Much of the color in this combination comes from the accent plants. The impatiens' small splash of violet and the light color of the trailing *Dichondra* 'Silver Falls' contrast well against the dark, rich blue the container.

combination 62

a *Impatiens hawkeri* 'Divine Cherry Red' (New Guinea impatiens) (M)

b *Coleus* 'Kong Mosaic' (U)

c *Dichondra* 'Silver Falls' (T)

d *Pennisetum glaucum* 'Jester' (ornamental millet) (U)

difficulty Moderate   **light** Part sun

container 14-inch, round, footed, lightweight urn

comments This container loves the heat and provides vibrant colors for a part sun area. The color of the New Guinea impatiens glows brilliantly and brings out the red in the coleus, while the bronze container brings out the bright, warm tones of the New Guinea impatiens.

tip For a different look, remove the ornamental millet and replace with *Alocasia* 'Williams' or *Alocasia plumbea* 'Nigra'. This will make this combination perfect for the shade.

combination 63

a *Eragrostis* 'Wind Dancer' (U)

b *Alternanthera* 'Purple Knight' (U)

c *Impatiens hawkeri* 'Divine Pink' (New Guinea impatiens) (M)

d *Coleus* 'Kong Rose' (M)

difficulty Moderate

container 14-inch, round ceramic

light Part sun

comments *Alternanthera* 'Purple Knight' can grow to be 16 to 20 inches tall, can spread 2 to 3 feet, and has striking, dark purple foliage.

tip Substitute *Coleus* 'Kong Red' for 'Kong Rose' or *I. hawkeri* 'Divine Mystic Mix' for 'Divine Pink'. Keep 'Wind Dancer' in check with occasional trimming.

combination 64

a   *Impatiens* 'Fanciful Red' (M)

b   *Impatiens* 'Fanciful Coral' (M)

c   *Coleus* 'Wizard Velvet Red' (U)

d   *Dichondra repens* 'Emerald Falls' (T)

difficulty   Moderate

container   14-inch, round, footed stone urn

light   Shade

comments   This container provides bright colors for the shade and is perfect for a summer or autumn event. *D. repens* 'Emerald Falls' will trail up to 3 feet and does well in both sun and shade.

tip   Substitute *Coleus* 'Wizard Coral Sunrise' or 'Wizard Mosaic' for 'Wizard Red Velvet'.

combination 65

a   *Pelargonium* x *hortorum* 'Designer Scarlet' (zonal geranium) (U)

b   *Tagetes* 'Durango Yellow' (marigold) (U)

c   *Petunia* 'Suncatcher Trailing White' (M/T)

d   *Carex* 'Toffee Twist' (U)

difficulty   Easy

container   14-inch by 10-inch, oval, cast-iron urn

light   Sun

comments   This combination is quick and offers easy elegance; the urn itself even makes a statement. *Carex* 'Toffee Twist' may look dead but do not be fooled. It is very much alive and makes a stunning accent to this elegant container.

tip   Plan to put the urn in a location where you will want to leave it, as it is quite heavy.

combination 66

a *Pelargonium peltatum* 'Galleria Snowfire' (ivy geranium) (U)

b *Plectranthus* 'Nico' (T)

c *Angelonia* 'Angelmist Lavender' (U)

d *Impatiens* 'Fanfare Fuchsia' (M)

difficulty Easy   **light** Sun

container 12-inch, round, lightweight fiberglass

comments The attractive, dark green leaves of *Plectranthus* 'Nico' will fill in all the empty spaces of your container garden. You will love the rich look of this accent plant. It does well in sun or shade and will grow 8 to 10 inches tall. The combination of the impatiens playing off the bicolored geranium is perfectly matched.

tip Substitute *Alternanthera* 'Purple Knight', *Angelonia* 'Angelmist Purple', *Angelonia* 'White', or *Angelonia* 'Pink' for *Angelonia* 'Angelmist Lavender'.

combination 67

a *Begonia* 'Dragon Wing Pink' (U/M)

b *Coleus* 'Kong Red' (M)

c *Alocasia* 'Polly' (U)

d *Rumohra adiantiformis* (leatherleaf fern) (M/U)

difficulty Moderate

container 16-inch, round, lightweight fiberglass

light Shade

comments The items in this container garden seem to be big, bigger, and biggest. You will enjoy boldness in conjunction with beauty and ease with this combination. *Alocasia* 'Polly' is an exciting and unusual accent that stands up to the big, bold coleus and begonia.

tip Substitute *Begonia* 'Dragon Wing Red' for 'Dragon Wing Pink', or try a different *Coleus* 'Kong' color instead of 'Kong Red'.

combination 68

a *Chamaedorea elegans* (Neanthe Bella palm) (U)

b *Perilla* 'Magilla' (U)

c *Dichondra* 'Silver Falls' (T)

d *Impatiens* 'Fanciful Sweetheart Mix' (M)

difficulty Moderate

container 16-inch, round stone

light Shade

comments Bring the palm tree indoors to enjoy throughout the winter months, but remember to wipe down all the leaves to make sure you are not bringing any unwanted insects inside.

tip Substitute the soft pink and white colors of *Impatiens* 'Fanciful Sweetheart Mix' with the bolder reds and corals of 'Fanciful Salsa Mix'.

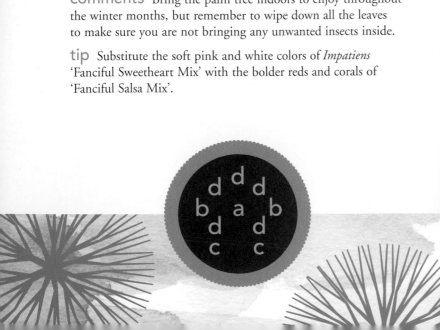

combination 69

a *Impatiens* 'Fiesta Coral Bells' (double impatiens) (M)

b *Impatiens* 'Fusion Glow' (exotic impatiens) (U/M)

c *Pennisetum setaceum* (fountain grass) (U)

d *Lotus* (lotus vine or parrot's beak) (T)

difficulty Moderate

container 14-inch, square, tall ripple ceramic

light Part shade

comments Lotus adds an unusual yet fun wispy look that complements the texture of the fountain grass.

tip For a more vibrant look, replace *Impatiens* 'Fusion Glow' with 'Fusion Red', 'Fusion Heat' or 'Jungle Gold'.

combination 70

a *Pelargonium* x *hortorum* 'Fantasia Flame Improved' (zonal geranium) (U)

b *Coleus* 'Kong Mosaic' (M)

c *Lysimachia* 'Goldilocks' (T)

d *Lantana* 'Lucky Pot of Gold' (T)

difficulty Easy

container 8-inch, conical coco fiber hanging basket with stand

light Sun

comments *Lysimachia* 'Goldilocks' is a perennial, hardy in Zones 3 through 10, and can be replanted in an area that needs a groundcover. The unique-looking, lightweight, conical stand can be moved easily to any location. If you decide you would like to use it simply as a hanging basket, the stand removes with no effort at all.

combination 71

a *Perilla* 'Magilla Purple' (U)

b *Impatiens* 'Pixie Pink Bicolor' (mini-impatiens) (M)

c *Impatiens walleriana* 'Fiesta Apple Blossom' (double impatiens) (M)

d *Artemesia* 'Silver Mound' (M)

difficulty Easy   light Shade

container 16-inch, terra-cotta-like, plastic color bowl

comments *Perilla* 'Magilla Purple' can be aggressive and get rather large, so you may need to cut it back. *Artemesia* 'Silver Mound' is a perennial, hardy in Zones 3 though 8. *Impatiens* 'Pixie Pink Bicolor' will grow to be about 8 to 10 inches tall.

tip If you prefer the look of double impatiens, then substitute *Impatiens* 'Pixie Pink Bicolor' with 'Pixie Double Sparkler Burgundy'. This rose flower form adds the brightness of white combined with burgundy petals.

combination 72

a *Colocasia* 'Illustris' (U)

b *Impatiens hawkeri* 'Celebrette Wild Plum' (New Guinea impatiens) (M)

c *Torenia* 'Clown Rose' (M)

d *Coleus* 'Kong Mosaic' (M)

difficulty Easy

container 14-inch, round stone

light Part shade/part sun

comments The tropical look of *Colocasia* 'Illustris' really adds impact to this container garden with both height and rich color.

tip For brightness, the *Torenia* 'Clown Rose' can be replaced with 'White Blush'. You may also substitute *Coleus* 'Kong Mosaic' with any other 'Kong' color.

combination 73

a *Leucanthemum* 'Snow Cap' (U)

b *Dianthus* 'Amazon Rose Magic' (U)

c *Angelonia* 'Angelmist Deep Plum' (U)

d *Sesleria autumnalis* (autumn moor grass) (U/M)

difficulty Easy   **light** Shade

container 12-inch, round terra-cotta

comments *Leucanthemum* 'Snow Cap' is a perennial, hardy in Zones 4 through 8. *Dianthus* 'Amazon Rose Magic' reaches 18 to 36 inches in height. It is perfect as a cut flower and attracts butterflies. Blooms on the dianthus will start out white and then turn to pink and then deep rose as they age. You will find all three colors present at one time on each flower head.

tip Substitute *Angelonia* 'Angelmist Deep Plum' with pink, dark pink, or dark rose. If you select *Angelonia* 'Angelmist Basket Purple', the habit of the flower changes from upright to mounding and trailing. Either habit will look nice.

combination 74

a *Petunia* 'Wave Lavender' (M/T)

b *Dichondra* 'Silver Falls' (T)

c *Plectranthus* 'Silver Shield' (T)

d *Eragrostis* 'Wind Dancer' (U)

difficulty Moderate

container 24-inch, round, lightweight fiberglass

light Sun

comments This container will make a really big statement thanks to the aggressive nature of the plants. With very little effort this container garden will have really big impact wherever you decide to display it. The front entrance to your home is a good choice. Keep *Eragrostis* 'Wind Dancer' and *Plectranthus* 'Silver Shield' in check by trimming with scissors.

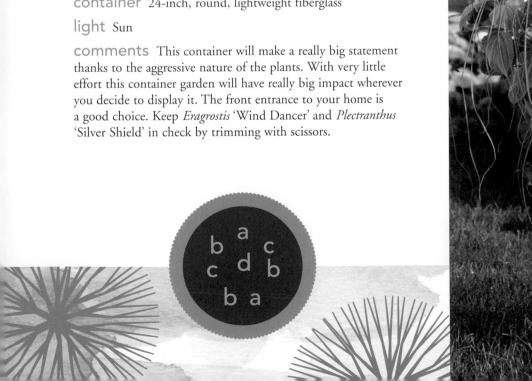

combination 75

a *Petunia* 'Suncatcher Purple' (M/T)

b *Pelargonium* × *hortorum* 'Allure Lilac Chiffon' (zonal geranium) (U)

c *Scaevola* 'Amethyst' (T)

d *Talinum paniculatum* (jewels of Opar) (U)

difficulty Easy   **light** Sun

container 14-inch, round ceramic

comments The blooms and berries of *T. paniculatum* will continue throughout the summer. This plant adds a totally different, almost outer-space-like look to your container garden. The chartreuse leaf color of *T. paniculatum* complements the shades of pink in this container.

tip You can substitute *Petunia* 'Wave Purple' for 'Suncatcher Purple', or add another *P. hortorum* 'Allure Lilac Chiffon' to the container for more blooms and more color.

combination 76

a *Helichrysum* 'Silver Mist' (M/T)

b *Dichondra* 'Silver Falls' (T)

c *Spilanthes* 'Peek-a-Boo' (M/T)

d *Iresine* 'Purple Lady' (T)

difficulty Moderate

container 14-inch, round clay

light Part sun

comments No need to worry about blooms or deadheading in this foliage container—just enjoy!

a b
d c d
b a

combination 77

a *Eragrostis* 'Wind Dancer' (U)

b *Tagetes* 'Marvel Orange' (marigold) (U)

c *Browalia* 'Blue Bells' (M)

d *Petunia* 'Wave Purple' (T)

difficulty Moderate

container 16-inch, round fiberglass

light Sun

comments This container has a wild and crazy look. Be careful not let the large or aggressive varieties take over the *Browalia* 'Blue Bells.' The large blooms of 'Marvel Orange' marigold make a stunning accent against the *Browalia* and petunia.

tip You can substitute a tamer, more controlled grass, like *Pennisetum* 'Rubrum' or 'Jester' (ornamental millet), for the *Eragrostis* 'Wind Dancer.'

combination 78

a *Impatiens* 'Fanfare Fuchsia' (M/T)

b *Helichrysum* 'Licorice Splash' (T)

c *Setcreasea* 'Purple Queen' (U/T)

d *Nemesia* 'Aromatica White' (U/M)

difficulty Moderate   **light** Shade

container 14-inch, round, coco fiber wire basket on stand

comments Having the container on a stand allows you to add height to any area of your garden. This works well when there are low-growing plants or perennials that are no longer in bloom. Or use as a backdrop when clustering containers on your deck or patio. *Impatiens* 'Fanfare Fuchsia' will not only mound and fill in the empty spaces of your container garden, but it will also trail over the side of the basket.

tip Bring the 'Purple Queen' indoors to enjoy throughout the winter.

combination 79

a *Iresine* 'Blazin' Rose' (U)

b *Sutera cordata* 'Abunda Giant White' (bacopa) (M/T)

c *Calibrachoa* 'Cabaret Red' (M/T)

d *Pelargonium peltatum* 'Colorcade White' (ivy geranium) (U)

difficulty Moderate   **light** Part sun

container 18-inch, round ceramic

comments Iresine can be aggressive, growing up to 10 to 30 inches. Use shears to cut it back or plant it in its own pot to keep it under control. If you prefer the look of geraniums over the look of bacopa, then replace one of the bacopas with an additional ivy geranium. *Calibrachoa* 'Cabaret' will grow 6 to 10 inches tall.

tip Display your container garden on another pot turned upside down to give it height and bring it closer to the eye. Substitute *Calibrachoa* 'Cabaret Red' with 'Cabaret Apricot' or 'Starlette Sunset'.

a a
c d d c
b b

combination 80

a *Begonia* 'Baby Wing White' (U/M)

b *Hedera helix* 'Glacier White' (variegated ivy) (T)

c *Cyrtomium falcatum* (holly fern) (U)

d *Sansevieria trifasciata* (mother-in-law's tongue or snake plant) (U)

e *Hypoestes* 'Splash White' (M)

f *Impatiens hawkeri* 'Celebration White' (New Guinea impatiens) (M)

difficulty Moderate   **light** Shade

container 8- and 12-inch round glazed ceramic

comments *C. falcatum* is a perennial, hardy in Zones 6 through 10. It can grow up to 2 feet tall and spread up to 2 feet as well. *S. trifasciata*, commonly called mother-in-law's tongue, is a surprising addition to this container and can be brought indoors for the winter.

a c
   b
d
a

e e
f e

combination 81

a *Pentas* 'Butterfly Light Lavender' (U)

b *Helichrysum* 'Licorice' (T)

c *Ipomoea* 'Ace of Spades' (T)

d *Calibrachoa* 'Million Bells Cherry Pink' (M/T)

difficulty Moderate   light Sun

container 14-inch, round terra cotta

comments This container will do great in the heat of summer. *Pentas* 'Butterfly Light Lavender' grows from 12 to 22 inches tall and spreads 10 to 18 inches. Butterflies and hummingbirds are attracted to its small, star-shaped flowers. Be careful not to let the *Ipomoea* 'Ace of Spades' take over the smaller, delicate flowers of calibrachoa.

tip If you like the look of *Ipomoea* 'Ace of Spades' and think you would like to add an extra one to your container, better think again unless the only thing you want left in your container is this aggressive grower.

combination 82

a *Fuchsia* 'Firecracker' (U)

b *Xanthosoma atrovirens* 'Dwarf Green' (U)

c *Heuchera* 'Harvest Burgundy' (M)

d *Hedera* 'Glacier' (variegated ivy) (T)

difficulty   Moderate

container   14-inch, round, glazed ceramic

light   Part shade

comments   *Heuchera* 'Harvest Burgundy' is a perennial, hardy in Zones 4 through 9. It has intense burgundy-bronze foliage and will grow up to 7 inches tall and spread 12 to 16 inches. *X. atrovirens* 'Dwarf Green' is a tropical plant with an attractive bluish tint. It can reach a height of 1 to 2 feet.

a b
c   c
c
d
c

combination 83

a *Capsicum* 'Black Pearl' (ornamental pepper) (U)

b *Angelonia* 'Angelmist White Cloud' (U)

c *Verbena* 'Aztec Purple Magic' (T)

d *Dichondra* 'Silver Falls' (T)

difficulty Moderate

container 14-inch, square, glazed, ripple ceramic

light Sun

comments The container for this mixed garden is a real showstopper, as it is tall, narrow, and square with an attractive, rippling pattern.

tip Using ornamental accents can add height and interest to your container garden.

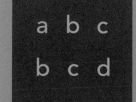

combination 84

a *Colocasia* 'Black Magic' (U)

b *Angelonia* 'Angelmist Dark Pink' (U)

c *Petunia* 'Easy Wave Shell Pink' (T/M)

d *Pennisetum setaceum* (fountain grass) (U)

difficulty Moderate

container 14-inch, square ceramic, 3 feet tall

light Sun

comments The dark smokey color of *Colocasia* 'Black Magic' complements the color of the container.

tip Any of the eight *Petunia* 'Easy Wave' colors will be a flattering addition to this combination.

d   a
   b
c   b

combination 85

a *Perilla* 'Magilla Purple' (U)

b *Catharanthus roseus* 'Titan Blush' (vinca) (U/M)

c *Helichrysum* 'Licorice' (T)

d *Pelargonium* × *hortorum* 'Designer Bright Lilac' (zonal geranium) (U)

difficulty Easy

container 12-inch, round, glazed ceramic

light Sun

comments *Perilla* 'Magilla Purple' and *Helichrysum* 'Licorice' can grow very large. Snip both back when they start to get too big for the size of the container or intrude on the other plants.

deck, patio, and garden 5

There is no better place to create a little space of your own to relax and enjoy your surroundings than your deck or patio. We spend a lot of time enjoying the great outdoors by barbequing, eating, and connecting with nature that it seems such a natural idea to decorate it just as we would a room inside our home. Outdoor decorations usually include furniture and accessories, just like any other room indoors. But your outdoor room can also contain color through the addition of container gardens. These smaller versions of your backyard garden are a great way to bring color and conversation to your outdoor living space. If you find a particular color to your liking, you can create your containers to include some or even all of that favorite color. The colors in your container garden can even match the fabric on your patio cushions or table umbrella. Displaying container gardens on your deck or patio will bring color and enjoyment all season long as well as invite butterflies, birds, and even your own friends to stop for a visit.

When you are going all out to plan an outdoor party—coordinating the theme, the dishes, the napkins, the furniture, and the food— container gardens can help you bring a theme to life or simply accent the color motif that you have created. Adding colorful container gardens can dress up the look and feel of any party, casual or formal. A quick tip: Add candles to your container gardens for an evening party. This can be done either with a candleholder inside an attractive hurricane or simply placed in the planter. The look is soft and beautiful, and if the candles are citronella you receive the added bonus of keeping away the mosquitoes.

You may consider bringing your herbs and vegetables to your backdoor in a container for easy access while you are preparing dinner. Why not containerize a tomato plant and reap the benefits of its many fruits? It is fun for young and old alike to watch these plants bloom and produce vegetables up close. If your container is large enough, you can even add a basil plant or two, giving you a ready-to-go salad when the tomatoes have ripened. Herbs of all types can be combined in a container garden. My container-grown parsley took first place at the local county fair three years in a row! Having herbs near your backdoor will also provide a wonderful scent all summer long. Do not forget that some herbs are perennials, so save a spot in your garden bed to transplant them before the summer is over or trim them back and bring the container indoors.

A container garden that is nestled within a garden bed can add height to low-growing plants or color to what might be a stalled or yet-to-bloom perennial garden. The beauty of having a container garden for your garden bed is that you can move it around anywhere you would like, constantly giving your garden a different look. Often we find the shade garden to be full of texture and shades of green in the middle of summer and lacking in any other color. A container garden can add just the right touch of color and will stand above all that texture, giving added height just by being planted in a container. One of my neighbors no longer plants annuals in her beds in front of her home. Instead, she assembles large combination planters and places them here and there, not on the front porch as you would expect, but nestled amongst her bushes and trees. They add just the right amount of color, and she did not even have to get on her hands and knees to plant, weed, or prune. When you are bored with the look of your garden, just move these containers around and you will have the feeling that your garden has been refreshed and renewed.

If you live in an apartment or condominium with only a balcony to garden on, container gardening allows you to have all the color and enjoyment of a garden without actually planting a garden bed.

There are so many ways to receive pleasure from container gardening. After all, isn't that what it's all about? Create a setting using your finished containers and other items such as chairs, fencing, large candleholders, etc. Surround yourself with the things you love. You will enjoy your outdoor setting as much as you do your favorite room inside. Move your containers around and add decorations to change the look, the feel, and the view of your outdoor sanctuary. There are many whimsical items for sale at your local garden center —you can find everything from ladybugs to frogs to angels to garden gods with names. These items come in plastic, stone, metal, wood, and wire and can add height or color to or simply accentuate your container garden. They are fun to have and can be used year after year. You can also find items on the clearance rack at your local department store at the end of the season or visit an antique or estate sale for similar items at a fraction of the cost.

The following container recipes usually incorporate at least five different varieties and range in complexity from easy to moderate. They are perfect for a deck, patio, balcony, or garden location.

combination 86

a   *Perilla* 'Magilla' (U)

b   *Pelargonium* x *hortorum* 'Showcase Light Lavender' (geranium) (U)

c   *Lamium* 'Jade Frost' (T)

d   *Nemesia* 'Aromatica Royal' (U)

e   *Jamesbrittania hybrida* 'Breeze White' (bacopa) (U)

difficulty Moderate   **light** Sun

container 24-inch, tin washtub

comments *Lamiastrum* 'Jade Frost' is a perennial, hardy in Zones 4 through 9, and can be replanted in your garden in the fall to be used the following year as a groundcover. Keep 'Jade Frost' looking great with an occasional trim.

tip You can add height to this container by displaying it on an overturned washtub.

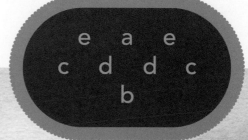

combination 87

a *Dahlia* 'Melody Latin' (U)

b *Catharanthus roseus* 'Titan Blush' (vinca) (U/M)

c *Ipomoea* 'Tricolor' (T)

d *Cordyline* 'Red Sensation' (U)

e *Pentas* 'Butterfly Deep Pink' (U)

f *Calathea tigrinum* (U/M)

g *Lantana* 'Landmark Rose Glow' (T)

difficulty Moderate   **light** Sun

container 16-inch, terra-cotta

comments This arrangement will attract butterflies. Deadhead the dahlia flowers when they are done blooming.

tip Substitute *Cordyline* 'Red Sensation' with dracaena spike. For more summer blooms, add any pink geranium.

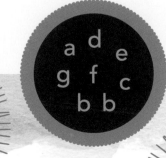

a   d
e
g f
c
b b

combination 88

a *Dichondra* 'Silver Falls' (T)

b *Impatiens* 'Super Elfin White' (M)

c *Begonia* 'Dragon Wing Pink' (U)

d *Coleus* 'Wizard Sunset' (U)

e *Iresine* 'Purple Lady' (T)

difficulty Moderate

container 14-inch, round stone

light Shade

tip For a brighter look, replace *Coleus* 'Wizard Sunset' with 'Wizard Rose'. Tone down the bulk of the container by replacing *Iresine* 'Purple Lady' with another *Impatiens* 'Super Elfin White' or *Dichondra* 'Silver Falls'.

combination 89

a   *Coleus* 'Kong Mosaic' (M)

b   *Iresine* 'Purple Lady' (T)

c   *Impatiens* 'Jungle Gold' (U)

d   *Begonia* 'Dragon Wing Pink' (M)

e   *Torenia* 'Clown Lemon Drop' (M)

f   *Dichondra* 'Silver Falls' (T)

difficulty Moderate

container 16-inch, round, lightweight fiberglass

light Shade

comments This combination provides great colors for the shade, and the light-colored container gives just the right brightness. Keep an eye on *Impatiens* 'Jungle Gold' and *Begonia* 'Dragon Wing' so that they do not take over *Torenia* 'Clown Lemon Drop'.

combination 90

a *Pelargonium* × *hortorum* 'Designer Violet' (zonal geranium) (U)

b *Verbena* 'Aztec Dark Purple' (T)

c *Helichrysum* 'Limelight' (T)

d *Coleus* 'Ducksfoot' (U)

e *Ipomoea* 'Blackie' (M/T)

difficulty Moderate

container 16-inch terra-cotta bowl

light Sun

comments This combination is filled with beautiful contrasting colors. Many of the varieties in this combination are trailers, so pick a spot where they can gracefully blend and trail, such as a wall. You can also try this combination in a hanging basket.

combination 91

a *Alternanthera* 'Ruby Red' (T)

b *Athyrium nipponicum* 'Pictum' (Japanese painted fern) (M)

c *Begonia* 'Constellation Capricorn' (M)

d *Impatiens hawkeri* 'Celebrette Wild Plum' (New Guinea impatiens) (M)

e *Phormium* 'Beyond Bronze' (U)

f *Impatiens* 'Fanfare Bright Coral' (M/T)

difficulty Moderate   light Shade

container 14-inch, round, terra-cotta-like plastic

comments *Athyrium nipponicum* 'Pictum' is a perennial, hardy in Zones 4 through 9. *Phormium* 'Beyond Bronze' has spiky leaves that are a light-copper color.

tip Replant the Japanese painted fern in your garden bed to enjoy again next year. It was chosen as the 2004 Perennial Plant of the Year.

f a
e a
b   d
c

combination 92

a *Codiaeum variegatum* (croton) (U)

b *Adiantum* (maidenhair fern) (M)

c *Begonia* 'Non-Stop Apricot' (M)

d *Ophiopogon japonicus* (mondo grass) (U)

e *Helichrysum* 'Silver Mist' (T)

difficulty Moderate

container 24-by-12-inch, rectangular ceramic

light Shade

comments These vivid colors will brighten any location. Accent with *Tillandsia usneoides* (Spanish moss) or *Dichondra* 'Silver Falls', or add a woven twig backdrop for height and attach a bromeliad for even more color. Maintain this look by giving the bromeliad an occasional spritz of water.

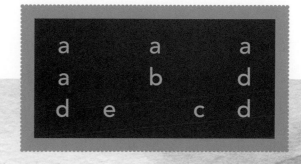

combination 93

a *Impatiens walleriana* 'Fiesta Pink Ruffles' (double impatiens) (M)

b *Bracteantha* 'Dreamtime Antique Shades' (M)

c *Begonia rex* 'Hilo Holiday' (M)

d *Vinca minor* 'Wojo's Jem' (T)

e *Matteuccia struthiopteris* (ostrich fern) (U)

difficulty Moderate

container 14-inch, round, terra-cotta-like plastic

light Part sun/part shade

comments Ostrich fern is a perennial; save it and plant in the garden at the end of the season. Although bracteantha really prefers the sun, I like to add this plant with its straw-like flowers because it reminds me of my mother. However, if you prefer something on the shady side, then substitute bracteantha with *Impatiens* 'Fusion Glow'.

combination 94

a *Pentas* 'Butterfly Light Lavender' (U)

b *Anethum graveolens* 'Fernleaf' (fernleaf dill) (U)

c *Dianthus* 'Bouquet Purple' (U)

d *Pelargonium peltatum* 'Summer Showers Burgundy' (ivy geranium) (T)

e *Artemesia* (wormwood) (U)

difficulty Moderate

container 14-inch, round terra-cotta

light Sun

comments *Dianthus* 'Bouquet Purple' is a perennial, hardy to Zone 4. This fragrant plant does well in the heat, reaches 18 to 24 inches tall, and is a great cut flower.

tip Substitute *Pelargonium peltatum* 'Summer Showers Burgundy' with 'Colorcade Violet' or Colorcade Burgundy Ice'.

combination 95

a   *Iresine* 'Blazin' Rose' (M/T)

b   *Musa* 'Zebrina' (banana tree) (U)

c   *Hedera* 'Glacier' (English ivy) (T)

d   *Pentas* 'Butterfly Lavender Shades' (U)

e   *Lantana* 'Landmark Yellow' (T)

difficulty Moderate

container 14-inch, round, glazed ceramic

light Sun

comments *Musa* 'Zebrina' and *Iresine* 'Blazin' Rose' both provide color to this container from their leaf color. *Iresine* 'Blazin' Rose' can be a bit large, so use your scissors to control it.

tip Add one or two additional *Pentas* 'Butterfly Lavender Shades' to the container to add more color.

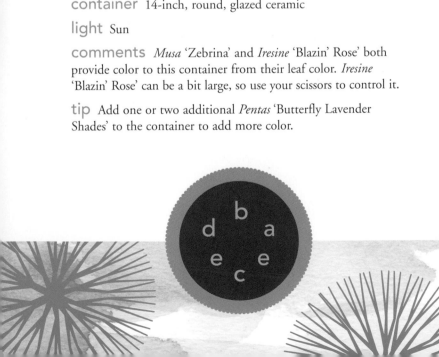

combination 96

a *Colocasia* 'Illustris' (U)

b *Capsicum* 'Black Pearl' (ornamental pepper) (U)

c *Pelargonium* x *hortorum* 'Designer White' (zonal geranium) (U)

d *Salvia* 'Mystic Spires' (U)

e *Calibrachoa* 'Cabaret Rose' (M/T)

f *Lysimachia* 'Goldilocks' (T)

difficulty Moderate

light Sun

container 14-inch, square ceramic

comments This is a tall, slender arrangement that will fit in any corner that needs a little color. *Colocasia* 'Illustris' combines green with a black haze to give this variety an attractive look. *Salvia* 'Mystic Spires' is a perennial, hardy in Zones 7 through 10. *Lysimachia* 'Goldilocks' is also a perennial, hardy in Zones 3 through 10. Transplant these into your garden at the end of the season.

b a b
c d
f e f

combination 97

a *Miscanthus* 'Porcupine' (U)

b *Coleus* 'Aurora Peach' (M)

c *Hedera* 'Thorndale' (English ivy) (T)

d *Pelargonium* × *hortorum* 'Showcase Scarlet' (geranium) (U)

e *Portulaca oleracea* 'Rio Orange' (purslane) (T)

difficulty Moderate to difficult   **light** Sun

container 18-inch, round, glazed ceramic

comments The bright color combination of the scarlet geranium and the orange purslane really heat up this mix. *Miscanthus* 'Porcupine' is a perennial, hardy in Zones 6 through 9.

tip If you're not crazy about the portulaca because the flowers open and close, then replace it with *Impatiens* 'Fanfare Bright Coral', *Calibrachoa* 'Cabaret Apricot', or *Lantana* 'Lucky Red Hot'.

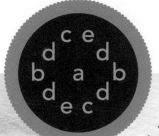

combination 98

a *Musa* 'Zebrina' (banana tree) (U)

b *Dahlia* 'Melody Swing' (U)

c *Helenium* 'Dakota Gold' (M)

d *Ipomoea* 'Ace of Spades' (T)

e *Lantana* 'Piñata' (T)

difficulty Easy

container 12-inch, round, glazed ceramic

light Sun

comments This container combination loves the heat.
Since this is a smaller container keep the *Ipomoea* under control
with an occasional trimming.

tip Bring *Musa* 'Zebrina' indoors to enjoy through the
winter months.

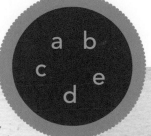

combination 99

a *Helenium* 'Dakota Gold' (M)

b *Catharanthus roseus* 'Titan Burgundy' (vinca) (U)

c *Vinca major* 'Variegata' (variegated vinca vine) (T)

d *Angelonia* 'Serena Purple' (U)

difficulty Easy

container Four-basket ladder

light Sun

comments This unusual plant stand looks like a ladder with four separate containers. You can plant each basket the same, or mix it up and enjoy a different view each time you turn the ladder. This arrangement can provide height in low-growing areas. The plan-o-gram on the left is planted on the upper left and lower right of the ladder, and the plan-o-gram on the right is planted on the upper right and lower left of the ladder.

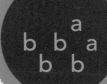

d d a
d a c
c

b b a
b b

combination 100

a *Begonia* 'Baby Wing Pink' (U/M)

b *Begonia* 'Baby Wing White' (U/M)

c *Hypoestes* 'Splash Pink' (M)

d *Hoya* (M/T)

e *Chamaedorea elegans* (Neanthe bella palm or parlor palm) (U)

difficulty Moderate

container 14-inch, round, lightweight fiberglass

light Part sun/part shade

comments Bring the hoya and the palm indoors to enjoy throughout the winter months. *Begonia* 'Baby Wing Pink' accentuates the soft-pink color in the hoya. *Hypoestes* 'Splash Pink' grows to be 10 to 18 inches tall and spreads 12 to 14 inches. It is also an attractive plant to bring indoors for a big splash of color without blooms.

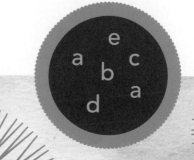

combination 101

a *Pennisetum glaucum* 'Purple Baron' (ornamental millet) (U)

b *Catharanthus roseus* 'Titan Lavender Blue Halo' (vinca) (U)

c *Pentas* 'Butterfly White' (U)

d *Petunia* 'Easy Wave Blue' (M/T)

e *Angelonia* 'Serena Purple' (U)

f *Dichondra* 'Silver Falls' (T)

difficulty Moderate

container 16-inch, round, lightweight fiberglass

light Sun

comments *Petunia* 'Easy Wave Blue' will fill in all the empty spaces and trail over the side of the container.

tip Substitute *Pennisetum glaucum* 'Jester' for 'Purple Baron', *Angelonia* 'Serena White' for 'Serena Purple', and *Dichondra* 'Emerald Falls' for 'Silver Falls'.

combination 102

a *Petunia* 'Easy Wave Pink' (M/T)

b *Lobelia* 'Periwinkle Blue' (M)

c *Dianthus* 'Purple Dynasty' (U)

d *Lantana* 'Landmark Rose Glow' (T)

e *Pennisetum setacetum* (fountain grass) (U)

f *Senecio cineraria* 'Cirrus' (dusty miller) (M)

difficulty Moderate   **light** Sun

container 12-inch, square terra cotta

comments *Dianthus* 'Purple Dynasty' is a perennial, hardy to Zone 6. It is lightly scented, grows to 16 to 20 inches tall, and makes a great cut flower. The dusty miller adds just the right amount of accent to this combination. If the lobelia stalls out in the heat of the summer, replace it with *Angelonia* 'Serena Purple'.

e c b

a d f

combination 103

a *Coleus* 'Kong Rose' (M)

b *Dichondra* 'Silver Falls' (T)

c *Impatiens* 'Fanciful Pink' (M)

d *Iresine* 'Purple Lady' (T)

e *Begonia* 'Dragon Wing Red' (U)

difficulty Moderate

container 14-inch, round, lightweight fiberglass

light Shade

tip If you like the look of tiny roses, then replace the *Impatiens* 'Fanciful Pink' with *Impatiens walleriana* 'Fiesta Apple Blossom' (double impatiens). *Begonia* 'Dragon Wing Red' can also be replaced with 'Dragon Wing Pink'.

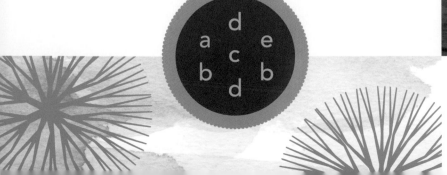

combination 104

a   *Musa* 'High Color Mini' (dwarf banana) (U)

b   *Pennisetum setaceum* (fountain grass) (U)

c   *Plectranthus* 'Silver Shield' (M/T)

d   *Iresine* 'Purple Lady' (T)

e   *Angelonia* 'Angelmist Lavender Stripe' (U)

f   *Phormium* 'Dusky Chief' (U)

difficulty Moderate   **light** Sun

container 14-inch, round, glazed ceramic

comments Bring this container indoors to enjoy through the autumn and into the winter months. *Angelonia* 'Angelmist Lavender Stripe' may stall out or die back, but the rest of the container will do just fine. Save *Musa* 'High Color Mini' and bring it indoors to reuse next year in your containers or garden bed.

combination 105

a   *Pennisetum glaucum* 'Purple Baron' (ornamental millet) (U)

b   *Helichrysum* 'Silver Mist' (M/T)

c   *Dichondra* 'Silver Falls' (T)

d   *Alternanthera* 'Purple Knight' (U)

e   *Petunia* 'Wave Rosy Dawn' (T)

difficulty   Moderate

container   Antique beet processor

light   Sun

comments   This beet processor is probably the most unlikely item that you would choose to create a container garden, yet it all comes together beautifully in a whimsical way.

tip   If you prefer more color, then *Tagetes* 'Sweet Cream' (marigold) would fit well with its large, creamy, white blooms and height of 16 inches.

combination 106

a *Miscanthus* 'Zebrinus' (U)

b *Coleus* 'Wild Lime' (U)

c *Coleus* 'Florida Sun Splash' (U)

d *Ipomoea* 'Marguerite' (ornamental sweet potato vine) (T)

e *Vinca major* 'Maculata' (vinca vine) (T)

difficulty Moderate

container 16-inch, grass-lined, wire basket on a raised stand

light Sun

comments *Miscanthus* 'Zebrinus' is a perennial, hardy to Zone 5. The beautifully striped leaves of this plant add just the right accent to this container garden and can grow up to 6 feet tall. If you are worried about height, then plant the grass in its original container and add it to your perennial bed at the end of the season. *Coleus* 'Florida Sun Splash' is a personal favorite because it produces a tremendous amount of color without a single bloom.

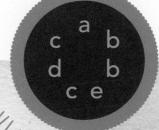

combination 107

a *Begonia* 'Baby Wing White' (U/M)

b *Begonia* 'Baby Wing Pink' (U/M)

c *Dichondra* 'Silver Falls' (T)

d *Iresine* 'Purple Lady' (T)

e *Coleus* 'Wizard Coral Sunrise' (U)

difficulty Moderate

container 12-inch, round, plastic, footed urn

light Shade

comments Easy elegance is achieved in this totally carefree container garden. This container will bring a lot of beauty and color to your shade garden.

tip Substitute *Coleus* 'Wizard Coral Sunrise' with *Coleus* 'Burgundy Red Ruffles', 'Florida Sun Rose', or 'Florida Sun Splash'.

combination 108

a *Colmanara* 'Wild Cat' (U)

b *Guzmania* 'Hilda' (bromeliad) (U)

c *Vriesea* 'Annie' (bromeliad) (U)

d *Hedera* (English ivy) (T)

difficulty Moderate

container 12-inch, round, bamboo container

light Shade

comments This totally tropical container can be enjoyed outdoors or in. Place it on a tray filled with stones and water to provide the humid environment all of the varieties prefer. An occasional misting with water helps as well. *Colmanara* 'Wild Cat' is very easy to grow and great for any beginner. It produces butterfly-shaped blooms and lots of them—it develops two to three flower spikes, and each spike produces up to 40 blooms.

b d b
c a a c
d b d

combination 109

a   *Talinum paniculatum* (jewels of Opar) (M/U)

b   *Pelargonium* x *hortorum* 'Designer Scarlet'
     (zonal geranium) (U)

c   *Capsicum* 'Black Pearl' (ornamental pepper) (U)

d   *Lantana* 'Lucky Peach' (T)

e   *Coleus* 'Wizard Golden' (U)

difficulty Moderate

container 12-inch, round fiberglass

light Sun

comments Three totally hot colors come together to make a big impact in this combination. 'Black Pearl' pepper will produce small, round, black peppers that will turn to red as they mature.

c   b   d
d   a   c
e   e
    b

combination 110

a *Duranta erecta* 'Variegated Mini Yellow' (M/T)

b *Calamagrostis* 'Eldorado' (U)

c *Geranium* 'Dusky Crug' (M)

d *Argyranthemum* 'Marguerite Madeira Crested Yellow' (U)

e *Coleus* 'Wizard Sunset' (U)

difficulty Moderate   **light** Sun

container 12-inch, round, glazed ceramic

comments *Calamagrostis* 'Eldorado' is a perennial, hardy in Zones 5 through 8, and *Geranium* 'Dusky Crug' is a perennial in Zones 4 through 8. The 'Dusty Crug' can be used as a groundcover when you remove it from your container garden in the autumn.

tip If *Argyranthemum* 'Marguerite Madeira Crested Yellow' stalls in the heat of the summer, replace it with *Tagetes* 'Marvel' (marigold) in a mix of gold, yellow, and orange, or *Coreopsis* 'Rising Sun'.

combination 111

a *Codiaeum variegatum* 'Victoria Gold Bell' (croton) (M)

b *Canna* 'Pretoria' (Bengal tiger) (U)

c *Lantana* 'Landmark Flame Improved' (T)

d *Coreopsis* 'Sunny Day' (U)

e *Impatiens hawkeri* 'Celebration Orange' (New Guinea impatiens) (M)

difficulty Moderate to difficult   **light** Sun

container 13-by-13-inch, square, short, plastic terra-cotta

comments *Coreopsis* 'Sunny Day' is a perennial, hardy in Zones 4 through 9. Even when not in bloom the striking leaves of *Canna* 'Pretoria' will put on a beautiful show. It can reach heights of 4 to 5 feet, and its bright orange blooms are the perfect complement to this mix. It can also be grown in water as an aquatic plant.

combination 112

a *Spilanthes* 'Peek-a-Boo' (T)

b *Coreopsis* 'Rising Sun' (U)

c *Helichrysum* 'Silver Mist' (T)

d *Alternanthera* 'Purple Knight' (U)

e *Tagetes* 'Durango Red' (marigold) (M)

f *Pennisetum glaucum* 'Purple Baron' (ornamental millet) (U)

difficulty Moderate   **light** Sun

container 14-inch, round, sand stone

comments This combination is perfect for the heat of summer. *Coreopsis* 'Rising Sun' is a perennial, hardy in Zones 4 through 9. *P. glaucum* 'Purple Baron' reaches a height of 2½ to 3½ feet. As the season progresses, the ornamental millet will produce attractive cattail-like flower plumes that will attract birds.

tip For more red, tuck two *Pelargonium* x *hortorum* 'Designer Scarlet' on each side of the millet. The addition of more red will help to accent the red centers of the 'Peek-a-Boo'.

combination 113

a   *Pelargonium* x *hortorum* 'Allure Tangerine' (zonal geranium) (U)

b   *Zinnia* 'Swizzle Scarlet Yellow' (U)

c   *Pennisetum setaceum* 'Rubrum' (purple fountain grass) (U)

d   *Calylophus* 'Yellow' (M/T)

e   *Iresine* 'Purple Lady' (T)

difficulty   Moderate

container   22-by-14-inch, oblong, aluminum bucket

light   Sun

comments   Deadhead the zinnia and zonal geranium to keep fresh blooms returning all season. Don't forget to drill drainage holes in your metal bucket before you plant.

combination 114

a *Begonia* 'Baby Wing White' (M)

b *Nephrolepis exaltata* (Boston fern) (U)

c *Caladium* 'Aaron' (U)

d *Hypoestes* 'Splash White' (M)

e *Impatiens hawkeri* 'Celebration White' (New Guinea impatiens) (M)

difficulty Moderate to difficult

container 18-inch, round, grass, wire basket on stone stand

light Shade

comments This combination, all in white, can go anywhere and will combine well with any other color combination or backdrop and will glow in an evening moonlit garden.

tip If you would like a trailer, add *Helichrysum* 'Licorice', *Dichondra* 'Silver Falls', or *Lamium* 'Jade Frost'.

combination 115

a *Begonia* 'Dragon Wing Pink' (M/T)

b *Hypoestes* 'Splash Red' (M)

c *Colocasia* 'Black Magic' (U)

d *Impatiens walleriana* 'Fiesta White' (double impatiens) (M)

e *Coleus* 'Wizard Velvet' (U)

difficulty Moderate to difficult

container 18-inch round on a pedestal

light Part sun/part shade

comments You can use two *Colocasia* 'Black Magic' for a lot of leaf power above the rest of the container. If you are afraid the begonia may overpower the hypoestes, you can eliminate the hypoestes completely; it won't affect the look of the combination.

tip Substitute *Begonia* 'Dragon Wing Pink' with 'Dragon Wing Red' or *Impatiens* 'Fiesta White' with 'Fusion Infrared' or 'Fanfare Bright Coral'.

a a
c
d   b
e
e
d — b

combination 116

a *Impatiens hawkeri* 'Celebration Frost' (New Guinea impatiens) (M)

b *Coleus* 'Kong Mosaic' (M)

c *Cordyline indivisa* (Dracaena spike) (U)

d *Begonia* 'Non-Stop Red' (M)

e *Dieffenbachia maculata* (U)

difficulty Moderate

container 12-inch, round, footed

light Shade

comments Bring the *Dieffenbachia maculata* indoors for the winter.

tip Substitute *Begonia* 'Non-Stop Red' with *Impatiens* 'Fiesta' Olé Purple' or 'Mini Pixie Purple'.

combination 117

a   *Athyrium* 'Felix Femina' (lady fern) (U)

b   *Impatiens walleriana* 'Fiesta Olé Frost' (double impatiens) (M)

c   *Coleus* 'Kong Rose' (M)

d   *Impatiens hawkeri* 'Celebration Electric Pink' (New Guinea impatiens) (M)

e   *Dichondra* 'Silver Falls' (T)

difficulty Moderate

container 14-inch, round stone

light Shade

comments *Athyrium* 'Felix Femina' is a perennial, hardy in Zones 4 through 8. The bright palette of the New Guinea impatiens will add a real burst of color to any partial shade or shade area.

hanging baskets 6

Hanging baskets are another form of container gardening. Just because the container is hanging from a hook instead of standing on the ground or on your table does not make it any less attractive or any less of a container garden. Hanging baskets can be planted to match your other combinations or can have their own look and style. They can be small and attractive or extremely large and showy. They can even add height to a cluster of containers to draw attention vertically for more impact. Select plants that are from the mounding and trailing category for the best results. If you include an upright variety, be certain that the size of the plant will not exceed the height of the hanger and that the basket can accommodate the maximum height the plant will reach. You can also include a climbing variety and train it to grow up the hanger as well as trail over the side.

Garden centers carry a wide selection of hanging baskets with a sphagnum, grass, or coir (coconut) fiber basket. Baskets can be bought in different shapes and sizes with the liner included or sold separately. Remember that these baskets will dry out much sooner than one that is made of plastic. They are, however, beautiful and are definitely worth the effort of watering them two or three times a day, if necessary. If your area is under watering restrictions due to a drought, look for basket liners that have a built-in water reservoir to help keep the plants and soil moist a bit longer. You can also choose a plastic container to reduce the amount of watering as they lose less water to evaporation.

Try hanging your basket from a tree branch or a shepherd's hook in your garden. If you are using a coco-lined basket and are not using trailing varieties, try adding slits to the side and planting additional plants. If your grass or coco basket is lined with plastic, make sure that you poke a few holes in the plastic for drainage.

Plastic tubes or sleeves (container 125) have become a popular way to hang a spot of color on a fence post, mailbox, or tree trunk. These flexible tubes are filled with potting mix, and plants are added to the pre-made slits. Simply hang and water. In no time you have a different-looking, very portable yet, beautiful container garden. Try hanging several end to end on the lower thicker branches or trunk of a tree. Wrap them around in a swirl to provide color in a most eye-catching way.

The following hanging basket recipes range from very simple with one or two varieties to difficult with an array of plants. Use these to discover how a hanging basket can bring your container gardening to a new level.

combination 118

a *Viola* 'Etain' (U)

b *Vinca major* (vinca vine) (T)

difficulty Easy

container 8-by-4-inch, painted, rectangular, metal
hanging basket

light Sun

tip With light yellow and lavender flowers, *Viola* 'Etain'
blooms profusely spring through autumn. This fragrant plant
is a perennial, hardy in Zones 4 through 8.

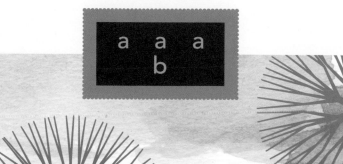

combination 119

a *Petunia* 'Easy Wave Shell Pink', 'Salmon', 'Rosy Dawn', 'Blue', 'Red', and 'White' (M/T)

difficulty Easy

container 18-inch, round, moss wire basket

light Sun

comments No need for pinching this beauty; it is totally self sufficient and only requires the necessities of life, such as food and frequent watering. Picking any or all the *Petunia* 'Easy Wave' colors that are available at your garden center and combining them in one basket creates a very festive and colorful look.

combination 120

a *Abutilon* 'Bella Mix' (U)

b *Lysimachia* 'Goldilocks' (T)

difficulty Easy

container 12-inch, plastic hanging basket

light Part sun/part shade

tip Substitute *Abutilon* 'Bella Mix' with any solid color available (i.e., red, pink, yellow, or vanilla) and *Dichondra* 'Silver Falls' or 'Emerald Falls' for *Lysimachia* 'Goldilocks'.

a
a a a
b

combination 121

a *Impatiens walleriana* 'Fiesta Olé Salmon' (double impatiens) (M)

b *Impatiens walleriana* 'Fiesta Olé Frost' (double impatiens) (M)

c *Coleus* 'Aurora Mocha' (M)

difficulty Easy

container 12-inch, terra-cotta-like, plastic hanging basket

light Shade

comments The dark, rich color of the *Coleus* 'Aurora Mocha' is a stunning backdrop to the *Impatiens* 'Fiesta Olé Salmon'. The addition of a splash of *Impatiens* 'Fiesta Olé Frost' on each side brightens the entire hanging basket.

tip Create a container garden using the same plan-o-gram to match.

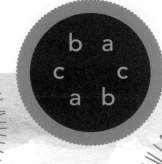

combination 122

a *Strobilanthes dyerianus* (Persian shield) (U)

b *Impatiens* 'Super Elfin Sunrise Mix' (M)

c *Fuchsia* 'Gardenmeister' (U)

d *Sutera cordata* 'Bridal Bouquet' (bacopa) (T)

difficulty Moderate

container 16-inch, round, grass-lined, wire hanging basket

light Shade

comments All of the plants in this container are top planted.

tip Substitute *S. cordata* 'Abunda Giant White' for *S. cordata* 'Bridal Bouquet' for larger blooms and real flower power. You can also make a matching container garden to sit on your deck or patio by using the same plan-o-gram.

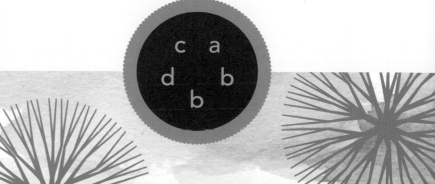

combination 123

a   *Pelargonium* x *hortorum* 'Allure Pink Sizzle' (zonal geranium) (U)

b   *Verbena* 'Aztec Silver Magic' (T)

c   *Petunia* 'Easy Wave Blue' (T)

d   *Hedera* (English ivy) (T)

difficulty   Easy

container   12-inch, wrought-iron, grass-lined hanging basket

light   Sun

comments   Add height and color to the seating area of your deck or patio with this smaller hanging basket.

tip   Any type of trailing ivy will work well in this combination. Try hanging the basket a little lower than most hanging baskets to enjoy all the flowers and the beautiful hanging basket up close.

combination 124

a *Impatiens* 'Fanciful Salmon' (M)

b *Impatiens* 'Jungle Gold' (U)

c *Abutilon* 'Bella Red' (U/M)

difficulty Difficult

container 24-inch, grass- and moss-lined hanging basket

light Shade

comments All of the varieties in this combination are top planted. The three lower accent containers have the following (L to R): *Impatiens* 'Jungle Gold' and *Iresine* 'Purple Lady'; *Coleus* 'Wizard Scarlet'; and *Dichondra* 'Silver Falls' and *Impatiens* 'Super Elfin Ruby'.

tip Side planting can be added for more color and to reduce the amount of grass that is visible. This can also be accomplished by adding a large trailing variety, such as *Ipomoea* 'Ace of Spades'.

a a c
c b b c
c a a

combination 125

a   *Dichondra* 'Silver Falls' (T)

b   *Impatiens* 'Super Elfin Lipstick' (M)

c   *Impatiens* 'Super Elfin Melon' (M)

difficulty   Easy

container   18-inch, plastic, hanging sleeve

light   Shade

comments   This is a different twist on hanging baskets. This sleeve can be hung from a tree, a fence post, or a hook.

tip   Put a couple sleeves that are in full bloom down the center of a table and tuck the hanger underneath for a different centerpiece. Water the sleeve ahead of time to prevent the table from getting wet.

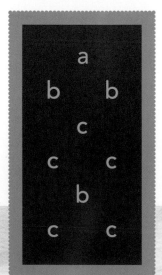

combination 126

a   *Impatiens hawkeri* 'Celebration Cherry Red Improved' (New Guinea impatiens) (M)

b   *Hosta* 'August Morn' (M)

c   *Ipomoea* 'Ace of Spades' (T)

d   *Athyrium* 'Pewter Lace' (M)

difficulty   Easy

container   14-inch, round, grass-lined hanging basket

light   Shade

comments   *Athyrium* 'Pewter Lace' is a perennial, hardy in Zones 5 through 8. The bright green leaves of *Hosta* 'August Moon' are a nice contrast when planted next to *Ipomoea* 'Ace of Spades'. Keep *Ipomoea* 'Ace of Spades' trimmed so that the basket will not get so heavy on one side that it becomes lopsided.

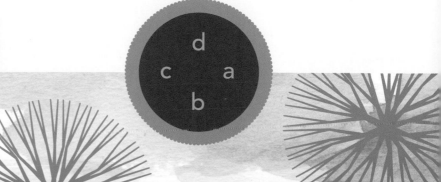

combination 127

a *Coleus* 'Aurora Black Cherry' (M)

b *Erygrostis* 'Wind Dancer' (U)

c *Duranta* 'Lime' (T)

d *Ipomoea* 'Marguerite' (T)

e *Argyranthemum* 'Madeira Deep Rose' (U)

f *Verbena* 'Aztec Wild Rose' (T)

difficulty Moderate to difficult

container 18-inch, round, grass-lined hanging basket

light Sun

comments *Argyranthemum* 'Madeira Deep Rose' carries you through the cooler temperatures of spring, and when the heat of summer really kicks in, *Verbena* 'Aztec Wild Rose' takes over and gives this hanging basket great color.

tip If you would like even more color in the spring, add *Calibrachoa* 'Cabaret Red'; in the summer add *Lantana* 'Lucky Red Hot'.

combination 128

a *Ipomoea* 'Marguerite' (T)

b *Verbena* 'Aztec Violet' (T)

c *Petunia* 'Wave Purple' (T)

d *Alternanthera* 'Purple Knight' (U)

e *Lamium* 'Jade Frost' (T)

f *Scaevola* 'Blue Ribbon' (T)

g *Strobilanthes dyerianus* (Persian shield) (U)

h *Plectranthus* 'Nico' (M/T)

difficulty Difficult   **light** Sun

container 18-inch wire, grass-lined hanging basket

comments Hanging baskets that are lined with grass can have side plantings, which provide additional interest and fullness to your hanging basket.

tip If the *Ipomoea* 'Marguerite', *Petunia* 'Wave Purple' or any of the other aggressive plants in this hanging basket start to become overgrown, just give them a haircut to keep them in control.

f b e
a d g d a
c b h

window boxes 7

Nothing adds a smile to your face quite like waking up and looking at a window box that frames your morning gaze upon your garden. It's like always having fresh cut flowers in your kitchen. Window boxes add a wonderful warm feeling to the facade of your home, increasing your curb appeal.

They are such beautiful additions to your home wherever they are placed. Do not limit yourself to adding window boxes to the base of your windows—they can be hung almost anywhere. Attach them to your deck railings, the side of your house, on a tree, or under a window—just about anywhere that can use a splash of color. How about over your garage doors? A watering wand should take care of your watering needs, and using a ladder every now and then will assist with any trimming or replacing necessary. Window boxes look great on the ground as well. In fact, anywhere that a round or square container garden can go, a window box can go too. Long or short, a window box will add color and fun anywhere you place it.

Window boxes can be made of wood and painted to match your home or shutters. They can be used year-round if you replace plants to suit each season. You can also use grass-lined baskets that have hooks on the back or purchase hangers that are specially made to easily hook on to your deck railing. Remember to make sure you take time to water these baskets more frequently to prevent drying out.

Yes, there is a bit of care that goes with the beauty that you will experience from your window box, but the small amount of time that it takes to tend to your container is well worth the effort. Fertilize and water with the same frequency that is used with your patio or deck container gardens, and snip or replace any items that begin to look a little tired. It's that simple.

combination 129

a *Pelargonium* × *hortorum* 'Patriot Cherry Rose' (zonal geranium) (U)

b *Vinca major* 'Variegata' (variegated vinca vine) (T)

difficulty Easy

container 9-by-27-inch, wooden window box with insert

light Sun

comments This is a great example of simple beauty.

tip If you prefer your geraniums to be in coral tones, substitute 'Patriot Cherry Rose' with 'Allure Tangerine', 'Fantasia Salmon', or 'Designer Peppermint Twist'. If you would like a white geranium to play off of the white variegation in the vinca vine, choose 'Designer White' or 'Fantasia White'.

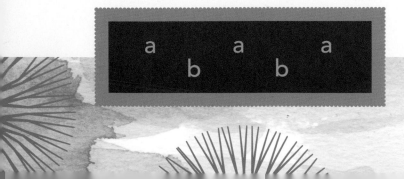

combination 130

a *Impatiens* 'Expo Cranberry' (M)
b *Iresine* 'Purple Lady' (T)

difficulty Easy

container 18-by-10-inch plastic, rectangular box

light Shade

tip Any color of impatiens will go great with *Iresine* 'Purple Lady'. Choose any of the twenty-eight *Impatiens* 'Expo' colors.

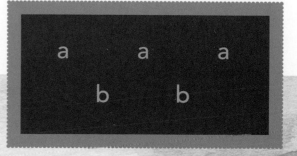

combination 131

a *Sutera cordata* 'Abunda Blue' (bacopa) (T)

b *Viola* 'Bingo Clear White' (pansy) (U)

c *Viola* 'Panola Deep Purple' (pansy) (U)

d *Osteospermum* 'Crescendo Orange' (U)

e *Felicia amelloides* 'Pinwheel Periwinkle' (U)

difficulty Moderate

container 18-by-10-inch, rectangular, wire and grass basket

light Sun

comments This is a great window box for the spring.

tip Substitute *Osteospermum* 'Serenity Pink' or 'Dark Lavender' for *Osteospermum* 'Crescendo Orange'.

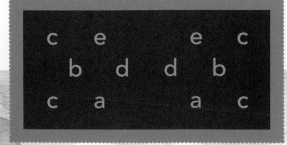

```
c   e       e   c
  b   d   d   b
c   c   a   a   c
```

combination 132

a   *Helianthus* 'Ballad' (sunflower) (U)

b   *Catharanthus roseus* 'Cooler Orchid' (vinca) (M)

c   *Iresine* 'Purple Lady' (T)

difficulty   Easy

container   36-by-12-inch, stone box

light   Sun

tip   Replace the sunflowers when they are done blooming with *Gaillardia* 'Torch', *Coreopsis* 'Sunfire', or *Hibiscus* 'Luna Blush'. *C. roseus* 'Cooler' is available in fourteen different colors and a mix. Choose lighter colors to bring brightness to the *Iresine* 'Purple Lady'. For a spicy-looking container, replace the vinca with *Capsicum* 'Medusa' (ornamental pepper).

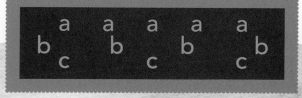

combination 133

a *Antirrhinum* 'Lampion Mix' (snapdragon)

difficulty Moderate

container 18-by-6-inch, rectangular, wooden window box

light Sun

comments There is no need to take time to select matching colors for this window box. The different colors mixed up together make a beautiful presentation and will be an eye-catcher, even from the street.

tip Bring the wooden box indoors at the end of the season, empty out the container mix, rinse, and dry before storing to prolong the life of the container.

combination 134

a *Dichondra* 'Silver Falls' (T)

b *Petunia* 'Dreams Rose Picotee' (U)

difficulty Easy

container 18-by-6-inch, rectangular, plastic

light Sun

tip *Petunia* 'Dreams Picotee' is also available in burgundy and red colors. The petunias also make a very attractive window box by themselves.

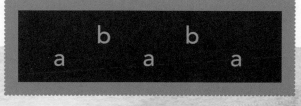

combination **135**

a *Impatiens* 'Jungle Gold' (U)

b *Dichondra* 'Silver Falls' (T)

c *Impatiens hawkeri* 'Tango' (New Guinea impatiens) (M)

d *Impatiens* 'Super Elfin Paradise Mix' (M)

e *Coleus* 'Wizard Jade' (U)

difficulty Moderate

container 36-by-12-inch, rectangular, wooden

light Sun

tip For an even bigger impact in a larger window box such as this one, replace *Dichondra* 'Silver Falls' with a broader leafed, more aggressive trailing variety, such as *Ipomoea* (sweet potato vine).

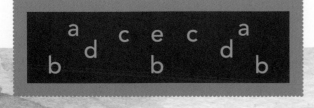

combination

a *Ocimum basilicum* 'Spicy Globe' (basil) (U)

b *Lavandula* 'Dutch Mill' (lavender) (U)

c *Ocimum basilicum* 'African Blue' (basil) (U)

d *Thymus vulgaris* (English thyme) (U)

e *Ocimum basilicum* 'Genovese' (basil) (U)

difficulty Moderate   **light** Sun

container 30-by-8-inch, rectangular, grass-lined window box

comments This herb combination is fragrant and will provide you with plenty of fresh herbs and sweet smells throughout the season. When summer is over, you can replant the herbs you like the best into smaller pots to bring indoors and put on you windowsill. If there are any perennial herbs, you can plant them in your garden for next year. For the remaining herbs, you can easily dry them by clipping at the base, tying the bundle together with raffia, and hanging the bundle upside down in your kitchen.

a b c d e

combination 137

a *Ipomoea* 'Blackie'
   (sweet potato vine) (T)

b *Carex* 'Toffee Twist'
   (sedge) (M)

c *Calibrachoa* 'Million Bells
   Crackling Fire' (M)

d *Ajuga reptans* 'Catlins
   Giant' (M/T)

e *Rosmarinus officinalis*
   'Salem' (rosemary) (U)

f *Rudbeckia* 'Cherokee
   Sunset' (U)

g *Rudbeckia* 'Indian
   Summer' (U)

h *Capsicum* 'Black Pearl'
   (ornamental pepper) (U)

difficulty Difficult

container 30-by-8-inch, rectangular, coir window box

light Sun/part sun

comments This window box incorporates perfect autumn colors. *A. reptans* 'Catlins Giant' is a perennial, hardy in Zones 3 through 9; *Rudbeckia* 'Cherokee Sunset' is a perennial, hardy in Zone 3 through 8; and *Rudbeckia* 'Indian Summer' is a perennial, hardy in Zones 7 through 10.

b e
c h f   g h c b
d   g   f a

combination 138

a   *Salvia officinalis* 'Aurea' (golden sage) (U)

b   *Salvia officinalis* 'Purpura-scens' (purple sage) (U)

c   *Lavandula augustifolia* 'Munstead' (English lavender) (U)

d   *Pennesitum setaceum* (fountain grass) (U/M)

e   *Catharanthus roseus* 'Titan Lilac' (vinca) (U)

f   *Pentas* 'Butterfly Lavender Shades' (U)

g   *Dichondra* 'Silver Falls' (T)

difficulty   Moderate   **light**   Sun

container   24-by-6-inch, rectangular, coir basket

comments   The purple and golden sages are perennials, hardy in Zones 6 through 9, while the English lavender is hardy in Zones 5 through 8. Not only will you be able to enjoy this container visually, you can also use the sage for cooking. Do not use chemical pesticides or fertilizers if you intend to cook with the sage. The lavender will provide fragrance from its flowers and leaves.

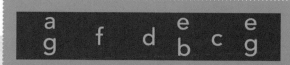

combination 139

a *Colocasia* 'Black Magic' (elephant's ear) (U)

b *Impatiens hawkeri* 'Celebration Rose Star' (New Guinea impatiens) (M)

c *Coleus* 'Kong Rose' (M)

difficulty Easy

container 8-by-22-inch, rectangular box

light Part sun/part shade

comments *Colocasia* 'Black Magic' will grow to be 4 to 6 feet tall. *Coleus* 'Kong Rose' is maintenance free with color that will last throughout the summer. Its leaves are large, and each plant can grow up to 18 to 20 inches tall.

tip Other *I. hawkeri* 'Celebration' colors that you can use are 'Sangria' and 'Rose'.

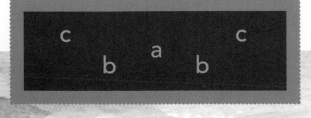

combination 140

a   *Angelonia* 'Serena Purple' (U)

b   *Hibiscus* 'Luna White' (U)

c   *Vinca* 'Cooler Red Rose' (U)

d   *Petunia* 'Easy Wave White' (T)

difficulty   Moderate   **light**   Sun

container   30-inch coco-lined wire hanging window box

comments   This is a wonderful Independence Day combination for a picnic or barbeque on your deck. *Hibiscus* 'Luna White' will stay compact but will provide you with large beautiful blooms all summer long. It is perennial to Zone 5—don't forget to remove it from the container at the end of the season and plant it in a garden bed so it will return next year.

tip   If you would like to change the look of this Fourth of July combination, then substitute *Hibiscus* 'Luna Pink Swirl' for *Hibiscus* 'Luna White' and *Vinca* 'Cooler Deep Orchid' for *Vinca* 'Cooler Red Rose'.

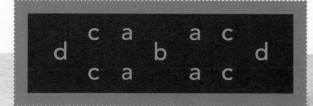

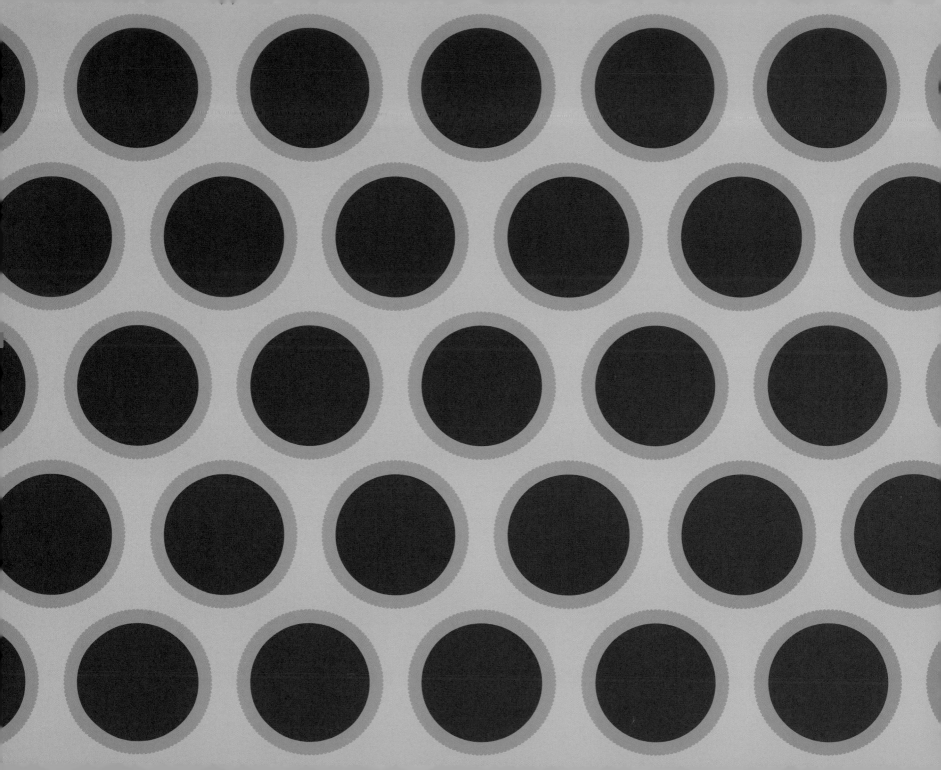

small, sweet, and sassy 8

Nothing adds beauty, fun, and color to your table like a small container garden. This little accent, whether it is a single color or variety or a combination of many, will make you smile every time you walk past, sit to enjoy a cup of early morning coffee, or share dinner with friends and family. Some combinations even add fragrance to your surroundings.

This is the easiest of all container gardens because you can use baskets, a watering can, or containers of any sort that are already in your home. Simply drop in a pot or two or three of your favorite flowers for an instant garden without any mess. Changing the look is equally simple by removing one plant and dropping in a fresh, new plant that offers a different look or color. If you need something inside the container to act as a filler or to help raise the height of the plant that you are dropping in pot and all, add an upside down plastic pot or scrunched up paper.

These plants can also be removed from the pot that you bought them in and planted directly into your basket or container. If you are using a basket that is lined with plastic, make sure that you cut a few slits in the bottom of the plastic to allow for drainage, otherwise your pots will be constantly sitting in water that could end up rotting the roots. If you would like to bring your basket or container indoors, do not forget to place a saucer or tray underneath to collect the water as it drains out and prevent water rings on your furniture. Since these are smaller containers you'll want to stay away from plants that trail. Instead rely on plants that will come up to or just over the edge of the container.

Unlike a bouquet of flowers that you throw away when you are ready to change the look on your table, you can plant your flowers in a garden bed or move the arrangement from the table to a windowsill, a nightstand, or outside on the deck.

These containers gardens are great for instant decorating. If you are planning a party that has a specific theme or colors, use varieties that will complement the table. Try ornamental peppers for a Mexican fiesta or the soft pink, white, and rose colors of *Dianthus* 'Sweetheart Mix' to set the mood for a romantic evening. Set a luncheon table using a plant in tiny terra-cotta pots at each place setting with the name of your guest inserted on a place card. This will not only direct your guests where to sit, but is also be a nice gift for them to take home and enjoy.

The combinations in this chapter may be small, but they make a big impact. The emphasis in these recipes is compactness and simplicity—ideal accents for tables, bedrooms, bathrooms, and windowsills. So, make a few, they're small but will provide hours of enjoyment.

combination 141

a *Petunia* 'Double Madness Lavender' (M)

difficulty Easy

container 8-by-8-inch, square, ceramic

light Sun

comments This container is the perfect complement to an afternoon tea or spring luncheon table. This petunia grows 10 to 15 inches tall and spreads 10 to 12 inches. The double petals of this petunia are as attractive as the petals of a rose.

tip Pick any on of the twelve *Petunia* 'Madness' colors available or select a mixture of your favorites.

combination 142

a *Aster* 'Pot 'n Patio Blue', 'Pink', 'Scarlet', and 'White' (M)

difficulty Easy

container 10-inch, octagonal, short terra-cotta

light Sun

comments This container beautifully dresses up a spring table indoors or out. This dwarf aster variety has double blooms, reaches a height of 6 inches, and spreads 6 inches. There's a lot of vibrant color wrapped up in this small plant.

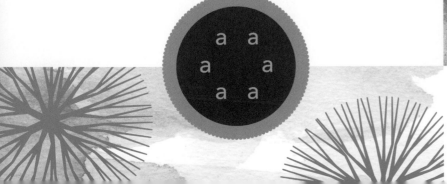

combination 143

a *Abutilon* 'Bella Mix' (U)

difficulty Easy

container 8-inch, round, short, glazed ceramic

light Part sun/part shade

comments This selection loves the heat but can also be brought indoors to add beautiful color to your table. The abutilon grows 14 to 18 inches tall and spreads 14 to 18 inches. Abutilon has tropical-looking papery blooms and multi-lobed maple-shaped leaves. It attracts butterflies and birds.

tip This abutilon variety is available in seven different colors as well as a mix.

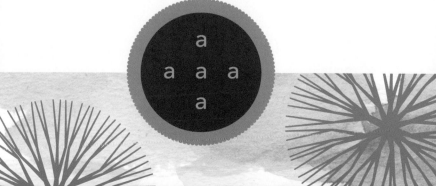

combination 144

a *Coleus* 'Wizard Mix' (U/M)

difficulty Easy

container 6-inch, metal watering can

light Shade

comments This coleus variety grows 12 to 14 inches tall and spread 10 to 12 inches.

tip If you cannot find *Coleus* 'Wizard Mix', look for any coleus in three different colors. Coleus has made a dramatic comeback over the last few years, and there are a number of colors and color combinations to pick from. Think coleus is just for the shade? Not anymore, which is why you need to read the plant tag before you purchase your coleus to make sure it is perfect for sun or for shade.

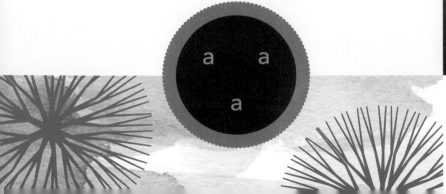

combination 145

a *Matthiola* 'Vintage Mix' (stock) (U)

difficulty Easy

container 8-inch, oval, woven basket

light Sun

comments This selection loves cooler weather and makes a pretty Easter basket for a friend. The fragrant stock grows 15 to 20 inches tall and spreads 12 to 14 inches. If you are using a plastic-lined basket, add drainage.

tip This stock variety is available in nine colors and two mixes. Try the 'Antique Mix' with its copper, peach, and yellow shades.

combination 146

a *Impatiens* 'Stardust Mix' (M)

difficulty Easy

container 6-by-6-inch, square wood

light Shade

comments This unusual-looking impatiens has a white star pattern in the middle and grows 8 to 10 inches high.

tip Use any combination of colors for a beautiful table display.

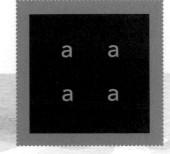

combination

a *Bellis* 'Bellisima Red', 'Rose', 'Rose Bicolor', and 'White' (U/M)

difficulty Easy

container 10-by-6-inch, oval, metal basket lined with plastic and sphagnum

light Sun

comments This plant is a perennial, hardy in Zones 4 through 8, and is perfect for the spring. It grows 6 to 10 inches tall and spreads 5 to 8 inches.

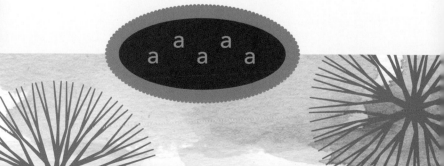

combination 148

a *Coleus* 'Wizard Pineapple' (U)

b *Lisianthus* 'Sapphire Pink Rim' (U)

difficulty Easy

container 8-by-6-inch, glazed ceramic with tray

light Sun

comments This combination does well in the heat and can be used as an indoor or outdoor container. *Coleus* 'Wizard Pineapple' grows to a height of 12 to 14 inches and a spread of 10 to 12 inches. *Lisianthus* 'Sapphire Pink Rim' has a pure, white flower with a touch of lavender-pink on the rim and grows to a height and spread of 4 to 6 inches.

tip You can use any color lisianthus in this container, depending on your décor needs.

combination 149

a *Coleus* 'Wizard Rose' (U)

b *Celosia* 'Glow Pink' (U)

c *Hypoestes* 'Splash White' (M)

difficulty Easy

container 10-inch, round basket

light Shade

comments The celosia grows from 10 to 12 inches tall and spreads 8 to 10 inches. If your basket is lined with plastic, add drainage.

tip Substitute *Celosia* 'Glow Pink' with 'Glow Red' for a richer effect or *Hypoestes* 'Splash White' with 'Pink' or 'Rose.'

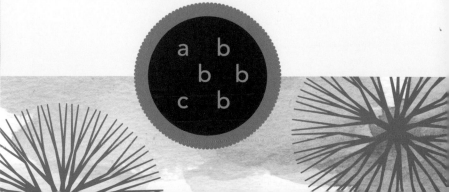

a b
b b
c b

combination 150

a   *Helianthus* 'Ballad' (sunflower) (U)

b   *Hypoestes* 'Splash Red' (M)

c   *Coleus* 'Wizard Jade' (U)

d   *Capsicum* 'Chilly Chili' (ornamental pepper)

difficulty   Easy

container   10-inch, round basket

light   Sun

comments   The plants in this combination can be dropped right in the basket still inside their pots. If the tops of the pots show, cover them up with a bit of sphagnum moss. *Hypoestes* is also known as the polkadot plant.

tip   Substitute *Hypoestes* 'Splash Red' with *Iresine* 'Purple Lady' or *Bracteantha* 'Dreamtime Copper'.

c   d

b   a

combination 151

a *Iresine* 'Purple Lady' (T)

b *Abutilon* 'Bella Yellow' (U)

c *Impatiens hawkeri* 'Divine White' (New Guinea impatiens) (M)

difficulty Easy

container 8-inch, round, glazed ceramic

light Part sun/part shade

comments The beautiful flowers of this abutilon resemble small hibiscus blooms.

tip Substitute *Abutilon* 'Bella Yellow' with pink or apricot shades.

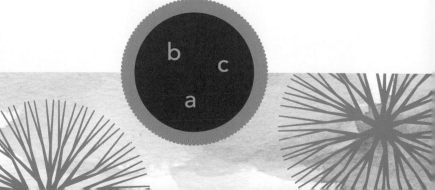

combination 152

a   *Sutera cordata* 'Abunda Giant White' (bacopa) (M/T)

b   *Verbena* 'Aztec Raspberry' (T)

c   *Perilla* 'Magilla Purple' (U)

difficulty   Moderate

container   8-inch, round, decorative, wooden basket

light   Sun

comments   Keep *Perilla* 'Magilla Purple' in control by planting it in its own pot. This plant can grow up to 36 inches tall.

tip   Adding sphagnum or grass to the top covers up the soil, helps retain moisture, and dresses up the look for your table.

combination 153

a *Helichrysum* 'Licorice' (T)

b *Lobelia* 'Waterfall Blue' (M)

c *Calibrachoa* 'Cabaret Hot Pink' (M/T)

d *Impatiens walleriana* 'Fiesta Olé Peppermint' (double impatiens) (M)

e *Hedera* (English ivy) (T)

difficulty Easy

container 10-inch, round, glazed ceramic

light Part sun

comments Indoors or out, this small ceramic pot filled with the soft colors of spring is charming. It makes a nice centerpiece for an outdoor table or as an accent on the deck or patio.

spring splendor 9

When that first breath of spring comes along in Chicago after a long, cold winter, you can always find me walking my garden to see if anything is poking its little head out of the ground yet. As a gardener, I receive a lot of excitement and pleasure at the first sight of anything returning from the following year. I become inspired enough to start carrying my containers out of their storage place in the garage to the backyard deck. This is a great time to remove and dispose of last year's soil if you did not do that in the fall and to check on the condition of your containers.

When the temperature reaches 60 degrees, I make my way to the local garden centers to take a look at all the new plants that are just begging me to plant them for spring, and I usually succumb to their call. Planting container gardens with those cute little violas and pansies, or items like phlox, snapdragons, and alyssum, is a wonderful way to welcome spring. Knowing how unstable this time of the year can be, planting your spring selections in a container allows you to easily bring the entire container indoors if the weather looks like it is going to reach freezing temperatures or to easily cover the container with a sheet for the night. It gives me a joyous feeling to get my hands in the dirt again and have living color on my deck by starting early with a spring container garden.

Color selections for spring are important. Pastels have soft shades yet make a very strong impact in the spring. You will want to stay with light pinks, yellows, and blues as well as white in the spring. How about a small Easter birdbath on the center of your dinner table combining the ever-popular yellows of daffodils and the purple shades of primroses? Or nestle a small stone rabbit in your container garden to celebrate spring.

The following recipes will add color to those first cool, spring days and herald the promise of the brighter, warmer days to come.

combination 154

a *Antirrhinum* 'Solstice Yellow' (snapdragon) (U)

b *Viola* 'Matrix Sunrise' (pansy) (M)

c *Diascia* 'Diamonte Coral Rose' (M)

difficulty Easy

container 16-inch, round, glazed clay

light Sun

comments This is a good choice for spring's cooler weather. *Viola* 'Matrix Sunrise' combines the delicate shades of yellow, peach, and rose and is the perfect complement to the *Diascia* and *Antirrhinum*.

tip The addition of bamboo or tree branches provides height and interest to your container, especially as a backdrop to these snapdragons. For smaller containers, use the same plan-o-gram but reduce the amount of each item.

combination 155

a   *Euphorbia* 'Diamond Frost' (poinsettia) (M)

b   *Juncus effusus* 'Quartz Creek' (U)

c   *Begonia elatior* 'Kenna' (M)

d   *Tulipa* (any 12-inch, red variety) (U)

difficulty Easy   **light** Part sun

container 12-by-24-inch picnic basket

comments Welcome spring with this whimsical, temporary, mixed container on a breakfast buffet.

tip Save the *Euphorbia* 'Diamond Frost' to add to a summer container garden.

b

c

d

d
a

c

combination 156

a *Viola* 'Sorbet Dark Blue Babyface' (M)

b *Viola* 'Sorbet Yellow Babyface' (M)

c *Phlox* '21st Century Blue' (U)

d *Lobelia* 'Regatta Rose' (M)

difficulty Easy   **light** Sun

container 12-inch, round fiberglass

comments This is a wonderful combination for cool, spring weather. The small-type phlox grows to be 10 inches tall. The tiny faces of the violas completely cover the plant. The lobelia reaches 6 to 8 inches tall, spreads 10 to 12 inches, and has a trailing habit.

tip Substitute *Phlox* '21st Century Blue Star' for '21st Century Blue'. *Lobelia* 'Regatta Rose' can be replaced with 'Regatta Lilac'. The delicate look of this combination fits perfectly into a hanging basket as well.

d a
b c b
a d

combination 157

a *Dianthus* 'Sweet Purple' (U)

b *Linaria* 'Enchantment' (U)

c *Viola* 'Matrix Yellow' (pansy) (M)

d *Lobularia* 'Easter Bonnet Violet' (alyssum) (M)

difficulty Moderate   **light** Sun

container 14-inch, round ceramic

comments Fragrant *Dianthus* 'Sweet Purple' reaches
a height of 18 to 36 inches and makes a great cut flower. The
pansy grows up to 8 inches in height, and its large blooms
can measure as much as 3 inches across. *Linaria* 'Enchantment'
is a delicate, wispy addition to the container garden with
bicolor blooms. It fits nicely in the secondary upright range
at 14 to 16 inches tall.

tip *Viola* 'Matrix' is available in fifteen colors and six mixes.
Also, the addition of tree twigs can add wonderful height to
your container.

combination 158

a *Viola* 'Matrix Ocean Breeze' (pansy) (M)

b *Delphinium* 'Guardian Blue' (U)

c *Delphinium* 'Guardian White' (U)

d *Aquilegia* 'Swan Blue and White' (U)

e *Nemesia* 'Poetry White' (M)

f *Nemesia* 'Poetry Lavender Pink' (M)

g *Lobelia* 'Riviera Midnight Blue' (M)

h *Delphinium* 'Guardian Lavender' (U)

difficulty Moderate

light Sun

container 16-inch, round terra-cotta

comments This great early-season container incorporates beautiful blues to welcome spring. *Aquilegia* 'Swan Blue and White' is a perennial, hardy in Zones 3 through 8, and *Delphinium* 'Guardian Blue' and 'Guardian White' are hardy in Zones 4 through 7.

tip For extra mid-level height, replace *Nemesia* 'Poetry White' with *Dianthus* 'Ideal White'.

combination 159

a *Viola* 'Matrix Primrose' (pansy) (M)

b *Dianthus* 'Ideal Select WhiteFire' (M)

c *Antirrhinum* 'Solstice Red' (snapdragon) (U)

d *Linaria* 'Enchantment' (U)

e *Lobularia* 'Snow Crystals' (alyssum) (M)

difficulty Difficult   **light** Sun

container 16-inch, round, glazed terra cotta

comments This container is ideal for cooler temperatures. The red glaze on the container complements the colors of this radiant red combination. *Antirrhinum* 'Solstice Red' is a knee-high snapdragon, reaching 16 to 20 inches tall, and is a great cut flower. The *Lobularia* and *Linaria* provide a heavenly fragrance.

tip Soften the look of this combination by using *Antirrhinum* 'Solstice Rose', 'Pink', or 'Yellow'.

combination 160

a *Viola* 'Matrix Blue Blotch' (pansy) (M)

b *Linaria* 'Enchantment' (U)

c *Dianthus* 'Ideal Select WhiteFire' (M)

d *Erysimum* 'Citrona Yellow' (U)

e *Diascia* 'Diamonte Lavender Pink' (M)

difficulty Moderate   **light** Sun

container 10-inch, round, glazed ceramic

comments This cool-temperature-loving container gives a burst of color for spring.

tip If you prefer to stay with rose shades, then replace *Viola* 'Matrix Blue Blotch' with 'Matrix Red Blotch' or 'Rose Blotch'. If you want to keep a hint of yellow, then *Viola* 'Matrix Sunrise' is a perfect fit. You may also substitute *Erysimum* 'Citrona Yellow' with *Phlox* '21st Century White'.

combination 161

a   *Viola* 'Sorbet Purple Babyface' (M)

b   *Lobelia* 'Riviera White' (M)

c   *Antirrhinum* 'Snapshot Plumblossom' (snapdragon) (U)

d   *Viola* 'Matrix Rose Blotch' (pansy) (M)

difficulty Easy

container 10-by-6-inch, oval stone

light Sun

comments This combination does great in the spring. *Antirrhinum* 'Snapshot Plumblossom' is a gorgeous bicolor snapdragon that combines perfectly with the extra-large blooms of *Viola* 'Matrix Rose Blotch'.

tip This container looks great as a springtime table centerpiece.

combination 162

a *Diascia* 'Diamonte Coral Rose' (M)

b *Helichrysum* 'Silver Mist' (M/T)

c *Viola* 'Panola Orange' (pansy) (M)

d *Erysimum* 'Citrona Yellow' (U/M)

e *Pennisetum glaucum* 'Jester' (ornamental millet) (U)

difficulty Moderate   **light** Sun

container 12-inch, round, lightweight stone

comments This container is perfect for the spring or cooler weather. 'Citrona Yellow' adds a different texture to the container and grows 10 to 12 inches tall. 'Jester' will grow 3 to 4 feet tall, and as it matures, the foliage will change from chartreuse to a deep burgundy.

```
      a
  c       d
  b   e   d
      c
      a
```

combination 163

a   *Nemesia* 'Poetry White' (U)

b   *Nemesia* 'Poetry Lavender Pink' (U)

c   *Viola* 'Matrix White' (pansy) (M)

d   *Viola* 'Sorbet Ocean Breeze Mix' (M)

difficulty Easy

container 12-inch, round, fiberglass

light Sun

comments This is a perfect container for the cooler temperatures of spring. Add this soft and sweet combination to your deck or patio for a springtime celebration or to welcome visitors at your front door. To add brightness to the overall look, use a lighter colored container.

b d
d
a c b
c
d d

autumn allure 10

When the weather turns cooler and the trees start to display their multicolored finery, it's not the time to pack in all your containers and call it a season. Take advantage of the cooler weather by spending more time in your garden, planting fall crops, doing maintenance, and preparing your spring and summer containers for cooler temperatures. September is a great time to transplant. Dig up perennials and perennial herbs and add them to your garden. Annual herbs can be brought indoors to get a few more weeks' or months' growth and use before you finally give them up for the winter.

Autumn is the perfect time to refresh and renew your tired container gardens by using the warm tones that signal autumn. Rich colors convey harvest time. The best choices for this time of the year usually include the brown tones, orange, deep purple, and bright yellows.

Autumn is also a great time to celebrate holidays, like Halloween and Thanksgiving. Try new varieties that will wow your trick-or-treaters and dinner guests in your containers Yes, mums provide beautiful harvest tones to your table and porch, but what about shaking those mums up for Halloween by adding *Spilanthes* 'Peek-a-Boo'? *Spilanthes* is a wonderful little accent plant that has unusual-looking yellow flowers that are round with a dark center, giving the appearance of an eyeball—the perfect spooky accent.

The following recipes incorporate the breathtaking colors of autumn with hardy plants that can stand up to autumn's chillier snaps.

combination 164

a *Linaria* 'Enchantment' (U)

b *Viola* 'Matrix Sunrise' (pansy) (M)

c *Phlox* '21st Century Buttercream' (M/U)

difficulty Easy

container 12-inch, round, etched terra-cotta

light Sun

comments This combination loves the cool weather of autumn. The terra-cotta pot blends well with the reds of the flowers and the colors of autumn. *Linaria* is fragrant, and the intense magenta and gold-colored flowers look like tiny snapdragons.

c
b   a   b
c

combination 165

a *Pennisetum glaucum* 'Purple Majesty' (ornamental millet) (U)

b *Thunbergia* 'Susie Orange with Eye' (T)

c *Iresine* 'Purple Lady' (T)

d *Alternanthera* 'Purple Knight' (U)

difficulty Easy   **light** Sun

container 12-by-12-inch square

comments This tall, slender container attracts attention and fits perfectly into narrow spaces. *Thunbergia* 'Susie Orange with Eye' is a trailer that can grow to lengths of 6 to 8 feet! This combination can be planted in the summer and will continue to do great well into autumn.

tip The addition of a trellis at the back of the container will allow the *Thunbergia* to climb up as well as trail down the sides. This variety is also available in white and yellow and with or without the dark eye.

combination 166

a *Helianthus* 'Ballad' (sunflower) (U)

b *Pennisetum glaucum* 'Purple Majesty' (ornamental millet) (U)

c *Iresine* 'Purple Lady' (T)

d *Spilanthes* 'Peek-a-Boo' (T)

e *Helenium* 'Dakota Gold' (M)

difficulty Difficult

container 16-inch, round stone

light Sun

comments Don't worry about the size of the sunflower—this variety only reaches 24 to 30 inches in height. *Spilanthes* 'Peek-a-Boo' makes a nice touch for Halloween. The tall ornamental millet adds the perfect height and a dark, rich color.

combination 167

a *Pennisetum glaucum* 'Purple Majesty' (ornamental millet) (U)

b *Tagetes* 'Durango Bolero' (marigold) (M)

c *Tagetes* 'Durango Flame' (marigold) (M)

d *Spilanthes* 'Peek-a-Boo' (T)

e *Alternanthera* 'Purple Knight' (U)

f *Helichrysum* 'Silver Mist' (M/T)

g *Coreopsis* 'Early Sunrise' (U)

difficulty Difficult

light Sun

container 16-inch, round, lightweight fiberglass

comments Accent plants bring continuous color without blooms to this container. *Coreopsis* 'Early Sunrise' is a perennial, hardy in Zones 4 through 9.

tip Substitute *Helichrysum* 'Silver Mist' with *Helichrysum* 'Licorice' for a look that softer and less dense.

combination 168

a *Viola* 'Halloween II' (pansy) (U/M)

Pictured in the background are *Coleus* 'Wizard Jade', 'Sunset', and 'Golden' as well as *Viola* 'Trick or Treat'.

difficulty Easy

container 6-inch pumpkin

light Sun

comments Drop the grower pot of this festive black pansy into a ceramic or real pumpkin for an instant holiday arrangement that can be placed anywhere.

tip In a ceramic container, this arrangement makes a great hostess gift. For more Halloween color, substitute 'Halloween II' with 'Trick or Treat Mix'.

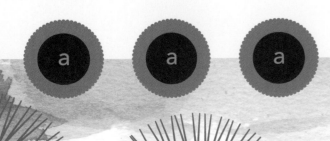

combination  **169**

a *Pennisetum glaucum* 'Purple Majesty' (ornamental millet) (U)

b *Spilanthes* 'Peek-a-Boo' (T)

c *Viola* 'Matrix White' (pansy) (M)

d *Erysimum* 'Citrona Yellow' (U)

difficulty Moderate

container 12-inch, round, glazed ceramic

light Sun

comments This combination incorporates great colors for the fall, and the eye-shaped flowers of *Spilanthes* 'Peek-a-Boo' add a delightful Halloween element.

tip Substitute *P. glaucum* 'Purple Majesty' with *P. glaucum* 'Purple Baron' or 'Jester' for a shorter upright variety. Add *Coleus* 'Florida Sun Splash' at the base of the ornamental millet to provide more mid-level height.

combination 170

a *Spilanthes* 'Peek-a-Boo' (T)

b *Chysanthemum* 'Ivory Time White' (U)

c *Brassica oleracea* (ornamental cabbage) (M)

d *Pennisetum setaceum* (fountain grass) (U)

e *Coleus* 'Wizard Velvet Red' (U)

f *Dichondra* 'Silver Falls' (T)

difficulty Moderate

container 16-inch, round, glazed ceramic

light Sun

comments There are so many unique varieties in this container that any side you view it from will look different.

tip Insert pheasant feathers to provide additional interest and dress up this container garden.

combination 171

a *Chrysanthemum* 'Onyx Time Yellow' (U/M)

b *Houttuynia cordata* (chameleon plant) (M/T)

c *Acorus gramineus* 'Oborozuki' (sweet flag) (M)

d *Thuja occidentalis* 'Emerald Green' (arborvitae tree) (U)

difficulty Easy

container 12-inch, round, glazed ceramic

light Sun

comments Plant the *T. occidentalis* 'Emerald Green' in your garden bed early enough to let the roots adjust to their new surroundings before harsh, winter weather arrives.

tip Snuggle a small pumpkin or an autumn-themed birdhouse in this container garden to make it really feel like a fall arrangement.

combination 172

a   *Heuchera* 'Plum Pudding' (M)

b   *Dryopteris erythrosora* (autumn fern) (U)

c   *Isolepsis* 'Live Wire' (M)

d   *Coleus* 'Rustic Orange' (U)

e   *Impatiens hawkeri* 'Celebration Orange' (New Guinea impatiens) (M)

difficulty Moderate

container 14-inch, round stone

light Shade

comments This container offers rich, autumn tones. *Heuchera* 'Plum Pudding' is a perennial, hardy in Zones 4 through 8, while the autumn fern is hardy in Zones 5 through 9. The addition of *Isolepsis* 'Live Wire' elevates this from a beautiful container to a "wow" container.

combination 173

a   *Dichondra* 'Silver Falls' (T)

b   *Heuchera* 'Harvest Burgundy' (M)

c   *Syngonium podophyllum* 'Exotic Charm' (Nephthytis) (U/T)

d   *Impatiens hawkeri* 'Celebration Bonfire Orange' (New Guinea impatiens) (M)

difficulty   Moderate

container   12-inch, round fiberglass

light   Part Shade

comments   *Heuchera* 'Harvest Burgundy' is a perennial, hardy in Zones 4 through 9. Bring the *Nephthytis* indoors to use as a houseplant throughout the winter.

simply grand 11

Are you the type of person that likes to do everything big, bold, and with flair? Or an individual that has to have the newest, the biggest, and the best? Or someone that likes to break all the rules? If any of these descriptions sound familiar, then this chapter is just for you. This is where you put it all together and let nothing get in your way. It is exciting to be able to find the perfect blend of color and texture and be able to match it up with the extravagant and to use an old standby in a new different way.

You will find that houseplants are not just about the house anymore. They have broken out of the backdoor to add wonderful texture with various shades of greens and burgundies to your shade garden. For example, remember that *Schefflera* that once graced the corner of your living room? Now a variegated variety adds height and an unusual, yet interesting, leaf structure to your container garden.

Do you want to rethink tropicals? Even if you do not live in Florida, the price of tropicals is so affordable that you can add them for color, texture, and height—not to mention excitement. I have a *Musa*, or banana tree, on my deck that is taller than my husband, and my whole family has had fun watching it grow and develop new leaves every few weeks. We are so fond of this tropical that I am sure we will have to find a home for it in our sunroom when the cooler, fall temperatures arrive.

Trying to attain a "simply grand" look is not difficult, as long as you remember the formula: Upright + Mounding + Trailing = A Beautiful Container. Incorporating each of these plant habits will always give you a container garden you will find delightful. Most anything that you can buy in your local garden center can be incorporated into a container garden: tree, shrubs, rosebushes. If there is a particular variety that is your favorite, then do not be afraid to add it. Have fun experimenting. Find what you like and what works best for you, and then grow it!

This is a chapter where anything and everything goes, and I hope you will have as much fun visualizing the possibilities as I have had sharing them with you. Use these wonderful combinations to spark your creativity and let it run wild!

combination 174

a *Begonia* 'Rhine Nadine' (M)

b *Hedera* 'Glacier' (ivy) (T)

c *Hydrangea* 'Nikko Blue' (M/U)

d *Adiantum capillus-veneris* (southern maidenhair fern) (M/T)

e *Caladium* 'White Christmas' (U)

difficulty Difficult

container 18-inch, round terra-cotta

light Shade

comments Plant the hydrangea in your garden for the winter, giving it time to take root, or bring the entire container indoors. Substitute the *Begonia* 'Rhine Nadine' with *Begonia* 'Non-Stop Yellow' for larger blooms and more color.

a b a
deced
a b a

combination 175

a *Pelargonium* x *hortorum* 'Designer Pink Parfait' (zonal geranium) (U)

b *Lobelia* 'Periwinkle Blue' (M)

c *Helichrysum* 'Licorice' (T)

d *Angelonia* 'Angelmist White' (U)

e *Ipomoea* 'Marguerite' (ornamental sweet potato vine) (T)

f *Pelargonium* x *hortorum* 'Designer Purple Rose' (zonal geranium) (U)

difficulty Difficult

container 18-inch, round terra-cotta

light Sun

comments This combination loves the heat. *Ipomoea* 'Marguerite' may need an occasional trim.

tip If *Lobelia* 'Periwinkle Blue' fades in the heat of the summer, replace it with *Angelonia* 'Serena Purple', *Verbena* 'Aztec Purple Magic', or *Boltonia* 'Jim Crockett'.

combination 176

a *Sutera cordata* 'Abunda White' (bacopa) (M/T)

b *Petunia* 'Suncatcher Pink' (M/T)

c *Angelonia* 'Angelmist White' (U)

d *Verbena* 'Aztec Pink' (T)

difficulty Moderate to difficult

container 24-by-24-inch, square, wooden box

light Sun

tip Double the amount of plants for a really grand-looking container. For additional height in the center, add *Colocasia* 'Black Ruffles', which will grow 4 to 6 feet tall, or *Colocasia* 'Excalibur', which is slight bit shorter. If you are crazy about blue, then replace *Petunia* 'Suncatcher Pink' with a combination of 'Suncatcher Sapphire' and 'Suncatcher Plum Vein', and *Verbena* 'Aztec Pink' with 'Aztec Violet'.

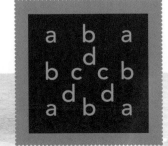

combination 177

a *Petunia* 'Tidal Wave Cherry' (U/T)

b *Dichondra* 'Silver Falls' (T)

difficulty Easy

container 16-inch, round, stone planter on a figurine pedestal

light Sun

comments The beauty of this container is simple, yet grand. The low-maintenance combination performs all summer long with only watering and fertilization necessary.

combination 178

a *Salix* (willow) (U)

b *Ipomoea* 'Ace of Spades' (T)

c *Plectranthus* 'Silver Shield' (T)

d *Pentas* 'Butterfly Deep Pink' (U)

e *Petunia* 'Double Wave Rose' (T)

f *Pennisetum setaceum* (fountain grass) (U)

g *Verbascum* 'Southern Charm' (U)

h *Petunia* 'Easy Wave Blue' (T)

difficulty Difficult   **light** Sun

container 20-inch, plastic terra-cotta

comments A tree in your container? Why not? Remember to give the container a properly weighted base before planting, or you will spend the summer trying to keep the entire container standing upright. Big plants in this hot summer container will make a big statement and complement the size of the willow.

a g
e f d h
e d d c
b

combination 179

a *Adiantum* (maidenhair fern) (M)

b *Hosta* 'Francis William' (U/M)

c *Begonia rex* (M)

d *Heucherella* 'Quicksilver' (M)

e *Torenia* 'Clown Violet' (M)

f *Impatiens* 'Super Elfin White' (M)

g *Heuchera* 'Purple Passion' (M)

difficulty Difficult　　　**light** Shade

container 16-inch, square, glazed ceramic

comments The warm gold tones in this container provide color for a shade garden and perfectly accent the plants in this mixed combination.

tip Transplant the hosta, fern, and heuchera in your garden bed for next year.

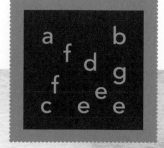

combination **180**

a *Pentas* 'Butterfly Light Lavender' (U)

b *Dichondra* 'Silver Falls' (T)

c *Eragrostis* 'Wind Dancer' (U)

d *Petunia* 'Wave Lavender' (T)

e *Plectranthus* 'Silver Shield' (T)

difficulty Moderate

container 14-inch, round, plastic, footed urn

light Sun

comments You'll love the soft blend of pink and silver in this container garden. Keep *Plectranthus* 'Silver Shield' in line with an occasional scissors snip. Butterflies love *Pentas*.

e
a   a
d   c   d
a
b   b

combination 181

a *Antirrhinum* 'Luminaire Trailing Yellow' (snapdragon) (M/T)

b *Calibrachoa* 'Starlette Trailing Rose' (M/T)

c *Angelonia* 'Angelmist Deep Plum Improved' (U)

d *Lobelia* 'Periwinkle Blue' (M)

Also pictured in the lower right is *Petunia* 'Tidal Wave Silver'.

difficulty Moderate

container 14-inch, round, tall stone

light Sun

tip For more height add, an ornamental grass, such as *Pennisetum glaucum* 'Purple Majesty', or a tropical plant, such as *Colocasia*. Substitute *Antirrhinum* 'Luminaire Pink' for 'Luminaire Yellow.' If *Lobelia* 'Periwinkle Blue' stalls out, then try replacing it with *Catharanthus roseus* 'Titan Lavender Blue Halo' or *Pentas* 'Butterfly Violet'.

combination 182

a *Pelargonium* x *hortorum* 'Fantasia Neon Rose' (zonal geranium) (U)

b *Diascia* 'Wink Pink' (M/T)

c *Perilla* 'Magilla Purple' (U)

d *Gaura* 'Ballerina Rose' (U)

e *Angelonia* 'Angelmist Light Pink' (U)

difficulty Difficult

container 12-inch, round clay

light Sun

comments If you love the color pink, then this container garden is for you. *Guara* 'Ballerina Rose' is a perennial, hardy in Zones 6 through 10. Its wispy flowers reach outward on their stems and seem to balance over the mixed container, adding a delightful touch.

tip *Diascia* 'Wink Pink' may stall or die back as the temperature rises. If that happens, just replace it with *Verbena* 'Aztec Wildfire Lavender Pink', *Petunia* 'Suncatcher Pink Vein', or *Petunia* 'Ruffle Pink'.

c d
a e
b b

combination 183

a   *Coleus* 'Kong Rose' (M)

b   *Caladium* 'Miss Muffet' (U)

c   *Impatiens hawkeri* 'Celebrette Sangria' (New Guinea impatiens) (M)

d   *Impatiens* 'Super Elfin Swirl Raspberry' (M)

e   *Fuchsia*, pink and purple varieties (M/T)

f   *Alternanthera*, bicolor variety (Joseph's coat) (M)

difficulty Moderate   **light** Shade

container 24-by-10-inch, oval ceramic

comments The color in this container comes primarily from the accent plants. The interesting shade of *Caladium* 'Miss Muffet' really stands out.

tip The addition of different levels of bamboo sticks adds height as well as an Asian flavor.

combination 184

a　*Calathea roseo-picta* (M)

b　*Impatiens hawkeri* 'Celebration Lavender' (New Guinea impatiens) (M)

c　*Hosta sieboldiana* 'Elegans' (M)

d　*Vinca major* 'Variegata' (variegated vinca vine) (T)

e　*Liriope muscari* 'Variegata' (U)

f　*Coleus* 'Dappled Apple' (U)

g　*Isolepsis* 'Live Wire' (M)

h　*Alternanthera* 'Purple Knight' (U)

difficulty Difficult　　**light** Shade

container 20-inch, round, stone pedestal

comments Save *C. roseo-picta* and bring it indoors to enjoy its attractive leaves throughout the winter. *H. sieboldiana* 'Elegans' can be planted in a garden bed and will return year after year. It has large blue-gray leaves and fragrant blooms, reaches 20 inches in height, and is slug resistant.

combination **185**

a *Lysimachia nummularia* 'Aurea' (T)

b *Coleus* 'Florida Sun Splash' (U)

c *Xanthosoma violaceum* (U)

d *Heuchera* 'Dolce Peach Melba' (M)

e *Impatiens hawkeri* 'Celebration Tropical Peach' (New Guinea impatiens) (M)

difficulty Difficult

container 18-inch, round stone

light Part Shade

comments *L. nummularia* 'Aurea' is a perennial, hardy in Zones 3 through 10, while *Heuchera* 'Dolce Peach Melba' is hardy in Zones 5 through 11 and features large, striking leaves that change from peach to orange in color. *X. violaceum* can grow 4 to 6 feet tall and has beautiful, dark-purple stems that really stand out.

combination 186

a *Begonia* 'Dragon Wing Pink' (U/M)

b *Coleus* 'Kong Mosaic' (M)

c *Plectranthus* 'Nico' (Swedish ivy) (T)

d *Alocasia gagaena* 'California' (U)

e *Impatiens hawkeri* 'Celebration White' (New Guinea impatiens) (M)

f *Impatiens hawkeri* 'Celebration Deep Red' (New Guinea impatiens) (M)

g *Hedera* 'Thorndale' (T)

h *Alternanthera* 'Purple Knight' (U)

difficulty Difficult

light Part shade/shade

container 24-inch, round stone

comments This is an incredibly large container that you will not want to move once it is in place. Each side of this container provides a completely different look from the next. *A. gagaena* 'California' adds good height to this combination, reaching 2½ to 3 feet with upright leaves. *Begonia* 'Dragon Wing Pink' and *Coleus* 'Kong Mosaic' and *Eragrostis* are larger plants that match the size of the large container.

combination 187

a *Impatiens* 'Fanfare Orange' (spreading impatiens) (M)

b *Impatiens hawkeri* 'Celebration White' (New Guinea impatiens) (M)

c *Hedera* 'Glacier' (variegated ivy) (T)

d *Alocasia gagaena* 'California' (U)

e *Nephrolepis exaltata* (Boston fern) (U/M)

difficulty Moderate

container 18-inch, round, plastic colorbowl

light Shade

comments This is such a fun, tropical look with beautiful height and color for the shade. *Alocasia gagaena* 'California' will grow as high as 2½ to 3 feet, so make sure you give it room to grow and use a sturdy container so the planting will not tip over.

combination 188

a *Athyrium* 'Pewter Lace' (nippon) (U)

b *Impatiens walleriana* 'Fiesta Olé Peach' (double impatiens) (M)

c *Ipomoea* 'Tricolor' (ornamental sweet potato vine) (T)

d *Begonia* 'Baby Wing Pink' (U/M)

e *Caladium* 'Carolyn Whorton' (U)

difficulty Moderate   **light** Shade

container 16-inch, round, glazed ceramic

comments The rich, red colors of the glazed-ceramic container are softly accented by the pink colors of the flowers and accent plants in this combination. *Athyrium* 'Pewter Lace' is a perennial, hardy in Zones 5 through 8. Plant this fern in a shady spot in your garden for the following year. *Caladium* 'Carolyn Whorton' is one of the most colorful caladium varieties available.

tip Substitute *I. walleriana* 'Fiesta Olé Peach' with 'Fiesta Apple Blossom', 'Fiesta Sparkler Cherry', or 'Fiesta Olé Peppermint'.

combination 189

a *Heuchera* 'Dolce Peach Melba' (M)

b *Heuchera* 'Licorice' (M)

c *Impatiens hawkeri* 'Celebrette Bonfire Orange' (New Guinea impatiens) (M)

d *Impatiens* 'Fusion Glow Improved' (M)

e *Alocasia plumbae* 'Nigra' (U)

f *Coleus* 'Wizard Coral Sunshine' (U)

g *Carex* 'Toffee Twist' (M)

difficulty Moderate

light Part shade

container 18-inch, round sandstone

comments This container is perfect if you want most of your color to come from foliage. *I. hawkeri* 'Celebrette Bonfire Orange' will add a small, yet ideal, amount of vivid color. *Heuchera* 'Dolce Peach Melba' is a perennial, hardy in Zones 5 through 11, and *Heuchera* 'Licorice' is a perennial in Zones 5 through 11. *A. plumbae* 'Nigra' has stunning, dark foliage and can grow 4 to 5 feet tall.

combination 190

a *Impatiens walleriana* 'Fiesta Olé Frost' (double impatiens) (M)

b *Begonia* 'Baby Wing White' (M/U)

c *Athyrium* 'Ghost' (U)

d *Hypoestes* 'Splash White' (M)

e *Begonia rex* 'Fairy' (rex begonia) (M)

difficulty Moderate

container 14-inch, round, glazed ceramic

light Shade

comments This combination will glow beautifully in a moonlit garden. *Athyrium* 'Ghost' is a perennial, hardy in Zones 3 through 8; plant it in your garden bed for the following year.

tip If you are having a difficult time finding *B. rex* 'Fairy', then substitute with any of the rex begonia varieties.

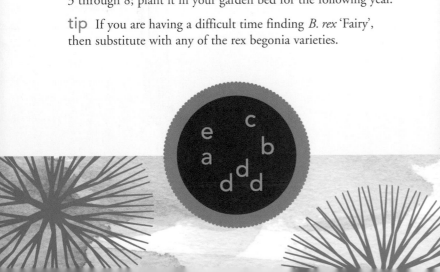

combination 191

a *Dahlia* 'Melody Gypsy' (U)

b *Pelargonium peltatum* 'Galleria Snowfire' (ivy geranium) (M/T)

c *Vinca minor* 'Variegata' (T)

d *Perilla* 'Magilla Purple' (U)

e *Petunia* 'Wave Purple' (T)

f *Stipa* 'Pony Tails' (M/T)

difficulty Difficult   **light** Sun

container 14-inch round on a pedestal

comments *P. peltatum* 'Galleria Snowfire' has a mounding, trailing habit and loves the heat. Keep *Petunia* 'Wave Purple' in line by snipping it back if it gets too long, since it can spread 3 to 4 feet in length. Don't forget to deadhead the dahlia and geranium to keep the blooms coming.

tip Substitute *Dahlia* 'Melody Gypsy' with 'Melody Lisa', *Petunia* 'Wave Purple' with 'Easy Wave Coral Reef', and *P. peltatum* 'Galleria Snowfire' with 'Galleria Bright Sunrise' for an entirely different look.

combination 192

a *Pennisetum orientale* 'Karley Rose' (oriental fountain grass) (U)

b *Pentas* 'Butterfly Lavender' (U)

c *Helichrysum* 'Licorice' (T)

d *Petunia* 'Suncatcher Plum Vein' (M/T)

e *Strobilanthes dyerianus* (Persian shield) (U)

f *Angelonia* 'Serena Lavender' (U)

difficulty Moderate

light Sun

container 14-inch, round, lightweight fiberglass

comments This is one of my favorite combinations. The softness of the fountain grass combines perfectly with the attractive plum petunias and the silver tones of the *Helichrysum*. *P. orientale* 'Karley Rose' produces rosy-lavender plumes, reaches 1 to 3 feet in height, and is a perennial, hardy in Zones 5 through 10. Persian shield adds a nice purple color and grows to be 18 to 24 inches tall.

combination 193

a   *Echinacea* 'Big Sky Sunrise' (U)

b   *Lavandula* 'Coco Dark Pink' (lavender) (U)

c   *Carex glauca* 'Blue Zinger' (M)

d   *Petunia* 'Suncatcher Plum Vein' (M/T)

e   *Lantana* 'Landmark Gold' (T)

f   *Heliotropium arborscens* 'Baby Blue' (heliotrope) (U)

difficulty Difficult   **light** Sun

container 16-inch, round, terra-cotta color blends

comments *Echinacea* 'Big Sky Sunrise' is a perennial, hardy in Zones 4 through 9; *Lavendula* 'Coco' is a perennial in Zones 7 through 9; and *C. glauca* 'Blue Zinger' is a perennial, hardy to Zone 5. *Echinacea* 'Big Sky Sunrisc' is a large, single daisy-like flower with citron-yellow petals and a green central cone that will mature to gold. It is slightly fragrant and attracts butterflies.

combination 194

a *Canna* 'Ermine White' (U)

b *Lantana* 'Lucky Pot of Gold' (T)

c *Coleus* 'Emerald Snow' (U)

d *Zinnia* 'Magellan Yellow' (U)

e *Alternanthera* 'Purple Knight' (U)

f *Calibrachoa* 'Terra Cotta' (T)

g *Libertia ixiodes* 'Taupo Blaze' (U)

h *Mentha* 'Chocolate Mint' (spearmint) (M/T)

difficulty Difficult   **light** Sun

container 16-inch, round fiberglass

comments *Mentha* 'Chocolate Mint' is very fragrant, spreads up to 36 inches, and is a perennial, hardy to Zone 4. *L. ixiodes* 'Taupo Blaze' adds a beautiful splash of color and texture to this mix.

tip Regularly deadhead the old zinnia flowers to encourage more blooms.

combination 195

a   *Mandevilla* 'Alice Du Pont' (U/T)

b   *Pelargonium* × *hortorum* 'Allure Pink Sizzle' (zonal geranium) (U)

c   *Hedera* 'Anne Marie' (English ivy) (T)

d   *Scaevola* 'Whirlwind White' (M/T)

e   *Zinnia* 'Magellan Pink' (U)

f   *Verbena* 'Aztec Cherry Red' (T)

g   *Angelonia* 'Serena White' (U)

h   *Petunia* 'Easy Wave Shell Pink' (T)

i   *Pennisetum setaceum* (fountain grass) (U)

j   *Artemisia* 'Powis Castle' (U/M)

difficulty Difficult   **light** Sun

container 16-inch, round fiberglass

comments Artemisia 'Powis Castle' is a drought-tolerant perennial, hardy in Zones 5 through 9, and can grow up to 30 inches tall. *P. setaceum* is a graceful, Hawaiian native and is very tolerant of dry conditions. It will grow 24 to 36 inches tall and is a perennial in Zones 8 through 10.

a b
e g e i
d g j h
f c

combination 196

a *Calibrachoa* 'Cabaret Purple' (T/M)

b *Petunia* 'Easy Wave White' (T)

c *Boltonia* 'Jim Crockett' (U)

d *Lavandula* 'Provence' (U)

e *Rosmarinus officinalis* (rosemary) (U)

f *Salvia* 'Mystic Spires' (U)

g *Pentas* 'Butterfly Deep Pink' (U)

difficulty Difficult   **light** Sun

container 14-inch round

comments This fragrant and functional container incorporates several perennials, including *Boltonia* 'Jim Crockett', hardy in Zones 4 through 9; *Lavandula* 'Provence', Zones 6 through 9; *Rosmarinus officinalis*, Zones 8 through 10; and *Salvia* 'Mystic Spires', Zones 7 through 10. *Salvia* 'Mystic Spires' sports true blue flowers all season long and grows 30 to 42 inches tall.

e
c f f
c c g b
a d

combination 197

a *Cyperus percamenthus* (U)

b *Colocasia* 'Black Ruffles' (U)

c *Eleocharis* 'Mountain Spikerush' (U)

d *Pontederia* 'Singapore Pink' (U)

e *Canna* 'Yellow' (U)

f *Echinodorus* 'Rose' (U)

difficulty Difficult   **light** Sun

container Large Frank Lloyd Wright water garden

comments *Colocasia* 'Black Ruffles' has intense, black scalloped leaves that will grow 4 to 6 feet tall and is a perennial, hardy to Zone 7. *Pontederia* 'Singapore Pink' has dark-green foliage with lavender-pink flowers that bloom all summer long and grows as tall as 24 inches. *Eleocharis* 'Mountain Spikerush' is a smaller, spiky aquatic, reaching 12 to 18 inches tall and has flower heads that resemble a paintbrush.

tip If you own an aquarium, *Echinodorus* 'Rose' doubles as an aquarium aquatic and grows 16 to 20 inches tall.

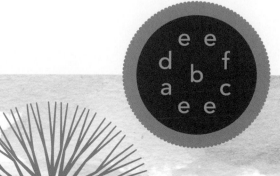

combination 198

a *Salvia officinalis* 'Aurea' (golden sage) (U/M)

b *Lavandula* 'Grosso' (lavender) (U)

c *Salvia officinalis* 'Berggartin' (sage) (U)

d *Plectranthus* 'Skeeter Skatter' (M/T)

e *Origanum vulgare* 'Aureum' (golden oregano) (T)

f *Origanum × majoricum* (Italian oregano) (T)

g *Salvia hybrida* (U)

h *Salvia officinalis* 'Tricolor' (sage) (U)

difficulty Moderate

light Sun

container Three round, terra-cotta bowls stacked, in sizes 14, 18, and 22 inches

comments Perennials in this container include: *S. officinalis* 'Berggartin', hardy in Zones 7 through 9; *Lavandula* 'Grosso', Zones 5 through 9; and *O. vulgare* 'Aureum' and *O. × majoricum*, Zones 5 through 9. *Lavandula* 'Grosso' blooms in summer and autumn and its fragrant flower spikes make great cut flowers. *S. officinalis* 'Berggartin' is a gourmet herb that can grow as tall as 24 inches. *O. vulgare* 'Aureum' can spread 9 to 12 inches.

combination 199

a *Delosperma cooperi* (M/T)

b *Delosperma congestum* (T)

c *Sedum repestre* 'Angelina' (T)

d *Delosperma floribundum* 'Sequins' (T)

e *Sempervivum tectorum* (hen and chicks) (M)

f *Kalanchoe* 'Donkey Ears' (U)

g *Sedum* 'Vera Jameson' (M/T)

h *Kalanchoe* 'Flapjacks' (M)

i *Sedum* 'Coral Reef' (M/T)

difficulty Difficult   **light** Sun

container 26-inch, round, shallow stone on a pedestal

comments This is the perfect container garden for areas with water restrictions. The following plants in this combination are perennials: *D. cooperi*, hardy in Zones 6 through 10; *S. repestre* 'Angelina', Zones 3 through 11; *Delosperma* 'Sequins', Zones 6 through 9; *Sedum* 'Vera Jameson', Zones 3 through 9; and *Sedum* 'Coral Reef', Zones 6 through 9.

combination 200

a *Coleus* 'Wizard Coral Sunrise' (U)

b *Coreopsis* 'Sunfire' (U)

c *Helenium* 'Dakota Gold' (M)

d *Abutilon* 'Bella Vanilla' (M)

e *Equisetum hyemale* (U)

f *Iresine* 'Purple Lady' (T)

g *Tagetes* 'Durango Outback Mix' (marigold) (U)

h *Rosmarinus officinalis* 'Tuscan Blue' (rosemary) (U)

i *Tagetes* 'Marvel Mix' (marigold) (U)

difficulty Difficult   **light** Sun

container 16-inch, round, footed plastic

comments *Coreopsis* 'Sunfire' is a perennial, hardy in Zones 4 through 9. The rosemary adds a bit of fragrance to this container garden. You can release its scent by gently rubbing the leaves between your fingers each time you walk past.

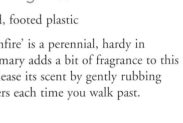

appendix

contact information

For additional information about the containers seen in this book, you can contact the following companies. These are wholesale companies, but they will be able to let you know who sells their products in your area.

Braun Horticulture
P.O. Box 160 Mount Hope
Ontario, Canada L0R 1W0
1-800-246-6984
www.braunhorticulture.com

Campania International
2452 Quakertown Road
Suite 100
Pennsburg, PA 18073
1-215-541-4627
www.campaniainternational.com

Garden City Plastics
89 Camms Road
Monbulk, VIC 3739
Australia
bob@gardencityplastics.com
www.gardencityplastics.com

New England Pottery/Norcal Pottery
1000 Washington Street
Foxboro, MA 02035
Contact your local garden center.
www.nepottery.com

Pride Garden Products
480 Shoemaker Road
Suite 101
King of Prussia, PA 19406
1-610-265-3977
www.pridegarden.com
www.aquasav.com

plant index

about the author

Sue Amatangelo is National Retail Accounts Manager at Ball Horticultural Company, West Chicago, Illinois. As part of that role she demonstrates at garden centers how to create and care for container gardens and stretches traditional container garden thinking to offer unique new container ideas in addition to the time-honored, foolproof recipes. Sue is a master gardener and winner of the Illinois Outstanding Master Gardener Award. She is also the Horticulture Superintendent of the Kane County, Illinois, Fair; Plan Commissioner for St. Charles; and a board member for Garden Centers of America. Sue and her family live in St. Charles, Illinois.